EFT for Christians—Tapping Into God's Peace .
book: *EFT for Christians*, is a wonderful book
to EFT, Christian or non-Christian, or simp.
peace and joy.

Although I have been a practitioner, teacher, and author of EFT for nearly 20 years, I increased my knowledge, understanding, faith, and gratitude for this amazing God-given tool exponentially by reading this brilliant book! Charity and Sherrie expertly explain the process, science, physiology, psychology, and related faith-based principles that are the synergistic wholeness of EFT. The case examples and scriptural references are superb. This book will be helpful to Christians and non-Christians alike to gain a uniquely personal understanding of their internal and external world, and how they can more easily create God's love, peace, and joy in their lives through EFT.

Dr. Kathleen A. Rick, BMS, MA, ACHt., EFT-Cert., CECP, DD
Author of the book: *A Guide to Energy Therapies for Counselors: Holistic Accelerated Healing Techniques to Complement Traditional Therapeutic Methods*

EFT for Christians—Tapping Into God's Peace and Joy should remove any doubt in a Christian's mind if tapping is for him or her. EFT is explained in terms that validate the usefulness of tapping with scriptural support to assure the Christian that EFT is indeed a gift from God. As explained in *EFT for Christians—Tapping into God's Peace and Joy*, tapping releases the blockages caused by traumatic events that years of prayer alone may not have been able to resolve. I see Christian EFT as a gentle, yet effective type of deliverance from painful memories and emotions that have prevented one from being free in Christ to being able to press in to God. A Christian may tap away because God is in the tapping.

Ronda Stone, ordained minister,
Women's Retreat Leader, Healing Rooms prayer ministry volunteer

As Christians, we strive for a closer relationship to God. Yet, many times this seems hopeless due to our sinful nature. In *EFT for Christians—Tapping into God's Peace and Joy,* Sherrie Rice Smith and Charity Virkler Kayembe outline a plan of action to break through the junk from our past that holds us back from this goal. They use the God given technique of EFT (Emotional Freedom Techniques). This is a "must read" for Christians who want to advance in their faith walk, lead a more Godly life, and experience the peace of Christ. EFT works!

Joy L. Druse BS, MS

I love this book! *EFT for Christians–Tapping into God's Peace and Joy* held my attention from beginning to end. Sherrie Smith writes with great passion, knowledge and experience. In this book she uses her spiritual perception to teach us that EFT is a tool of healing and "restoration to both the Church and to the dying world." Sherrie's books have been instrumental in helping me to understand and to integrate EFT into my Christian counseling practice. I have more than 20 years of experience as a Soul Physician, and EFT is an answer to my prayers. I thank God for using Sherrie to bring this message to the Christian world.

Janet Cook, Ph.D.
Director of Healing Streams Center LLC
Senior Pastor, River of Life Community Church in Elkhart, IN.
Email: janetcookphd@aol.com

As I began reading *EFT for Christians–Tapping into God's Peace and Joy*, I realized this was new territory for me. Having been in Inner Healing and Deliverance Ministries for more than 20 years, I seldom come across something "new." After reading a few chapters, I found myself cautiously intrigued by what I read. That's when I knew the Lord ministered to me. One Corinthians 12:4–6 describes the multifaceted nature of the Holy Spirit, His gifts, and His ministries. I became excited and realized this should happen often—new revelation and new teachings on the dynamic nature of God's Spirit. This book opened my heart to new avenues of healing. Great job, ladies!

Joe Brock, Sr. Minister,
Vineyard Assembly of God, Tipton, IN

EFT for Christians–Tapping into God's Peace and Joy is a "must have" for every Christian library. It uncovers and demonstrates in a practical, simplified way how to bring freedom to every soul that uses EFT. The book lays a foundation with science and testimonies—backed up by the Word of God.

Within minutes of finishing this book, I was able to apply its teaching and get a breakthrough in an area that had always "triggered" anxiety in me. That "trigger" is now gone. Thank You, Jesus. And thank you, Charity and Sherrie, for sharing this knowledge and revelation with the rest of the world.

Kurt Green
AS, BS, ND, CNHP
www.KurtGreen.org

EFT for Christians–Tapping into God's Peace and Joy is a direct gift from the Holy Spirit. It is not only a clinical guidebook to EFT, delving into the science and physiology of our Created selves, but it also a spiritual guidebook leading us to wholeness and freedom. It guides us along the path of Restoration to the very core of who we were created to be, by the One who is our creator.

Thank You, Charity and Sherrie, for the Blessing of *EFT for Christians–Tapping into God's Peace and Joy*. What a gift for my clients, family, friends and my own personal journey to wholeness!

Katherine Lehman ND, River's Edge Natural Health

This book is a wonderful sequel to Sherrie Rice Smith's first book. It provides strong science and solid technique with excellent case studies and supportive scripture. As a Christian therapist, I am looking forward to using this book to set the bar for standard of care in Christian EFT. I'm anticipating it will become a well used resource.

Debra Reid, MSW LCSW

I am so excited about this latest gift from Sherrie Rice Smith, author of the first *EFT for Christians*. In this new book, she gets down to the nitty-gritty of how to apply EFT in the world of the Christian believer. As a pastor of a Protestant church, you may find it unusual that I am interested in Emotional Freedom Techniques, or maybe not if you believe in Romans 8:27–28: "And He who searches our hearts know the mind of the Spirit because the Spirit intercedes for the saints according to the will of God. And we know that God works all things together for the good of those who love Him, who are called according to His purpose."

As a pastor and coach, I have discovered various healing modalities the Holy Spirit uses for our healing. I have used EFT many times within my ministry and coaching practice to help bring about God's peace and direction for those who are hurting. I am extremely pleased this book and the EFT discipline is now being made available to God's people.

Rev. Kymberley Clemons-Jones, MSEd, M.Div.
Pastor Valley Stream Presbyterian Church, Valley Stream, NY
Restorationlifecoach@gmail.com
restorationlifecoach.com

For those of us already convinced of the effectiveness of EFT—its method, science, and healing power—this book provides a solid summary of what makes it one of the most remarkable pathways toward healing and wholeness today. For those of us who are Christian, *EFT for Christians–Tapping into God's Peace and Joy* represents a bridge—a link—between a practice that is intrinsically spiritual with Christian theology, conviction and faith. Alongside *EFT for Christians* this important new book completes the one-stop reference library for Christians and EFT.

Rev. Dr. Timothy Carson
Senior Pastor of Broadway Christian Church, Columbia, Missouri.
Author of *Your Calling as a Christian*,
The Square Root of God, Six Doors to the Seventh Dimension,
and *Liminal Reality and Transformational Power*.

"I will give thanks to You, for I am fearfully and wonderfully made; Wonderful are Your works, And my soul knows it very well." (Psalm 139:14)

We are only now beginning to appreciate these astute words from King David. Truly we are wondrously made. Science is beginning to reveal the wonder of God's genius in the creation of the human body. Today enters a new chapter in this revelation. EFT (Emotional Freedom Techniques) uses the miracle of our creation, the wonder of our construction, to release tension, anxiety and worry.

EFT for Christians–Tapping into God's Peace and Joy will put a powerful tool into your own hands. You will no longer need to fear the shadows in the dark recesses of your mind, heart or past. The authors will lead you, in a non-threatening way, through a procedure that will allow you to very simply break free of anything that has ever tormented you. You can even wash away those unsettling emotions that are still lying in the pit of your stomach from your most recent meeting or phone call. Learn to survive life and to regain your peace and joy.

You were meant to live in the peace of the Lord. God even empowered your physiology with the ability to release joy into every fiber of your being. EFT is a tool, and you will want *EFT for Christians–Tapping into God's Peace and Joy* by Dr. Kayembe and Sherrie Rice Smith in your toolbox.

Pastor Ivey Rorie
Lewisville, NC
www.IveyMinistries.org

I am a neurosurgeon turned minister who has been given the opportunity to endorse Sherrie and Charity's book on Emotional Freedom Techniques, *EFT for Christians—Tapping into God's Peace and Joy.*

Basically, Emotional Freedom Techniques releases blocked energy that has accumulated as the result of emotional stress. This includes trapped pain and ungodly beliefs also known as self-inflicted nonsense, which can be resolved.

Emotional Freedom Techniques works because human beings have an energy system. EFT accesses this energy system in an amazing way and, therefore, should be in everyone's first-aid kit. The more I study EFT, the more fascinated I become.

Emotional Freedom Techniques is by far a most empowering tool because you can use it yourself and you can use it with others. And it's always available to you once you get the rhythm of it and choose where you want to go.

EFT for Christians—Tapping into God's Peace and Joy is a phenomenal book written for your understanding and training. This book is for anyone who wants to learn EFT from highly experienced people. The more you read, the more you'll learn, and the greater your response.

Rev. Phil Goldfedder, MD
HealingIsYours.com

EMOTIONAL
FREEDOM
TECHNIQUES

EFT FOR CHRISTIANS

TAPPING INTO GOD'S PEACE AND JOY

Foreword by **Dr. Mark Virkler**
President, Christian Leadership University

CHARITY VIRKLER KAYEMBE, PH.D.
AND SHERRIE RICE SMITH, R.N. (RETIRED)

True Potential
REACH THE WORLD

EMOTIONAL FREEDOM TECHNIQUES—EFT FOR CHRISTIANS
Tapping Into God's Peace and Joy

Cover and Interior Page design by True Potential, Inc.

ISBN: 978-1-943852-35-2 (paperback)
ISBN: 978-1-943852-36-9 (ebook)

Library of Congress Control Number: 2016952083

True Potential, Inc.
PO Box 904, Travelers Rest, SC 29690
www.truepotentialmedia.com

Printed in the United States of America.

Sherrie's Dedication

Thank you to my husband, Brad, who supports me every step of the way. Any more than I understood it, I don't think Brad knew what he was signing up for when he put that wedding ring on my finger 25 years ago!

Charity's Dedication

To my husband, Leo, the most peace-filled, joyful person I've ever known. Thank you for filling my world with love and laughter. I'm so grateful I get to do life together with you!

ACKNOWLEDGMENTS

Lord God, I thank You for guiding my every step, and thank You for sending us Jesus, Who is our healer. We surrender all that EFT is to Your almighty hands.

And to all you Christian EFT Practitioners and student Practitioners, thank you for your patience and deference with/to me as I step out here with God's help to bring EFT to the Christian world.

"For this reason, ever since I heard about your faith in the Lord Jesus and your love for all God's people, I have not stopped giving thanks for you, remembering you in my prayers." Ephesians 1:15–16

TABLE OF CONTENTS

FOREWORD

As a Christian, I believe that Jesus came to give us an abundant life filled with joy and peace. Yet, all too often, even sincere Christians go through life as "walking wounded." Abuse, trauma and negative experiences in our childhood live on in us into adulthood, shaping our character and damaging our health. Everyday pressures and irritations bring stress that settles into our very cells and challenges our faith. Thankfully, our Lord understands and He has provided us with many gifts of healings by which we can overcome and live in victory (see 1 Cor. 12:28). I am convinced that EFT is one of those healing gifts.

I am so grateful to Sherrie and Charity for their work in this important text. Sherrie brings a background in the medical field from her many years as a nurse that provides a solid scientific foundation for EFT. In addition, she has experienced the power of EFT to bring healing in her own life and has taught many others how to find relief both as an EFT practitioner and a teacher. Charity brings the theological and biblical foundation that we believers need to feel safe when we explore such new fields. Together they have given the Church another powerful tool to help the hurting and heal the wounded. What a wonderful gift!

I have experienced the power of EFT both in my own life and in my ministry. Not long after I began to learn about EFT, a relative made an offhand comment to me that pricked my heart like a thorn. I was hurt and I was angry. And within a few hours, the muscles in my shoulders were so tense that my neck became stiff and my head began to ache. Not good. Now, I know several ways to handle such situations but I decided to give EFT a try. Charity led me in several rounds of tapping and within minutes the tension was released, I had forgiven my relative and was able to laugh about the comment! I was sold – EFT works.

I now include EFT in my "divine healing toolbox" as one of the tools the Lord may lead me to use in my counseling ministry. It can touch and release issues that have been buried for decades, especially when used in conjunction with repentance, inner healing and godly confessions. I am pleased to introduce to you my friend Sherrie, my daughter Charity, and the healing gift from Jesus known as EFT.

Dr. Mark Virkler
President, Christian Leadership University

PREFACE
Disclaimer

Please read the following Disclaimer before proceeding further:

The information presented in this book, including, ideas, suggestions, exercises, techniques, and other materials, is educational in nature and is provided only as general information and is not medical or psychological advice. This book is solely intended for the reader's own self-improvement and is not meant to be a substitute for medical or psychological treatment and does not replace the services of licensed health care professionals.

This book contains information regarding an innovative healing method called Emotional Freedom Techniques or EFT which is considered part of the field of complementary and alternative medicine. EFT seeks to address stressors and imbalances within the person's energy system, as well as the energetic influence of thoughts, beliefs, and emotions on the body. EFT is intended to balance an individual's energy with a gentle tapping procedure. The prevailing premise of EFT is that the flow and balance of the body's electromagnetic and more subtle energies are important for physical, spiritual, and emotional health, and for fostering well-being.

Although EFT appears to have promising emotional, spiritual, and physical health benefits, EFT has yet to be fully researched by the Western academic, medical, and psychological communities. Therefore EFT may be considered experimental. The reader agrees to assume and accept full responsibility for any and all risks associated with reading this book and using EFT. If the reader has any concerns or questions about whether or not to use EFT, the reader should consult with his/her licensed health care professional. If the reader inadvertently experiences any emotional distress or physical discomfort using EFT, the reader is advised to stop and to seek professional care, if appropriate.

Publishing of the information contained in this book is not intended to create a client-practitioner or any other type of professional relationship between the reader and the authors. The authors do not make any guarantee that the reader will receive or experience the same results described in this book. Further, the authors do not make any guarantee, warranty, or prediction regarding the outcome of an individual using EFT as described herein for any particular purpose or issue. While references and links to other resources are provided in good faith, the accuracy, validity, effectiveness, completeness, or usefulness of any information herein, as with any publication, cannot be guaranteed.

By continuing to read this book the reader agrees to forever, fully release, indemnify, and hold harmless, the authors, and others associated with the publication of this book from any claim or liability and for any damage or injury of whatsoever kind or nature which the reader may incur arising at any time out of or in relation to the reader's use of the information presented in this book. If any court of law rules that any part of the Disclaimer is invalid, the Disclaimer stands as if those parts were struck out.

We, the authors, purposefully refer to satan with a lowercase "s." He was defeated at the Cross, leaving him bereft with no jurisdiction over our lives or emotions, thus he deserves no particular or special recognition.

BY CONTINUING TO READ THIS BOOK YOU AGREE TO ALL OF THE ABOVE.

INTRODUCTION

May the God of hope fill you with all joy and peace as you trust in him, so that you may overflow with hope by the power of the Holy Spirit! (Romans 15:13)

EMOTIONAL FREEDOM – IS IT REALLY THAT BIG A DEAL?

Emotional Freedom Techniques, or EFT, is an effective tool to accomplish precisely what its name implies: liberty and choice in regard to our feelings and how we experience them.

Scripture tells us we comfort others with the comfort we ourselves have received (2 Corinthians 1:3–5). In order for us to be a blessing to others, it is most helpful if we are not among the walking wounded. To the degree that we are healed and comforted, we can offer those same gifts much more freely to others.

Obviously, if I'm overwhelmed at work, stressed out in my relationships, worried about my finances, disappointed with God, afraid of the future, and feeling guilt-ridden in general, I don't have a lot of time or energy left to be considerate of the needs of those around me. I've got my own problems! How can I expect to help others, too?

When we are living in toxic emotions, we aren't the most effective ministers of the gospel of Jesus Christ. The word gospel actually means "good news." If I look at my life, is it a good advertisement for this Good News, for this Gospel of Peace? Am I living into the promises that the Bible says are mine? Am I experiencing righteousness, peace and joy in the Holy Ghost?

While these negative emotions don't serve us well, and in fact, greatly diminish and hinder our service to others, the opposite is also true. Positive feelings are the seedbed of greatness. If bad emotions are so wrong, then what about good emotions? Are they really that important?

FAITH WORKS THROUGH LOVE

Matthew 14:14 shows us how Jesus healed the sick out of compassion. He also ministered deliverance out of compassion (Mark 9:22), and fed the hungry out of compassion (Matthew 15:32). And He even spoke and taught the multitudes out of compassion (Mark 6:34). That's what motivated Jesus. Compassion is what moved Him.

So is compassion just a warm, fuzzy feeling? No, the picture God gives us through Jesus' life is clear: Compassion releases power. Compassion must be present in order to release healing and spiritual energy. It's not just a nice tingly feeling; it is the most powerful emotion in heaven and earth. These Scriptures clearly demonstrate the direct correlation between the divine emotion of compassion and the release of divine power.

Compassion is a "carrier wave" of God's power and grace. In telecommunications, a carrier wave is what the message (e.g., word, image, music, signal) is carried on. The message is encoded in the carrier wave by modifying the latter's frequency, amplitude, or phase.

Similarly, the divine frequency of compassion must be present for God's healing power to work; it is the wave upon which His grace is carried and released. Compassion is the "spiritual carrier wave" that conducts God's wisdom, healing, power, and gifts to us and through us to others.

Compassion is an emotion, and so is love. We are told the love of God should control and compel us (2 Corinthians 5:14). But is the Lord really that concerned with how we *feel*—good or bad, positive or negative? Where is His heart on all this?

WHAT'S LOVE GOT TO DO WITH IT?

When we first begin to practice EFT, we learn about the two-part "setup phrase." In the first part we acknowledge a negative emotion we're feeling. In the second part we affirm we love ourselves in spite of ourselves. For example, you will repeatedly hear some version of the setup phrase as, "Even though I feel (fill in the blank with a negative emotion)—I still deeply and profoundly love and accept myself." Sherrie will teach us in later chapters how the setup phrase is a prominent component of effective EFT sessions, especially in EFT for Christians.

SELF-LOVE. REALLY?

To personally explain the important principle of self-love, let's rewind a few years to a time when I was stuck. I had tried to learn and apply Scriptures about judgment such as, "Judge not lest you be judged." I also focused on the opposite of judgment, which I had understood to be love. I, therefore, committed the entire thirteenth chapter of First Corinthians to memory. I wanted to walk in love and not be critical!

Eventually, Holy Spirit got my attention and explained the root of my problem. I was being critical of someone and was feeling guilty for being critical. I prayed: "God, I know, I know. I need to love that person as I love myself."

God said, "No, please don't. The problem is you *are* loving your neighbor as you love yourself. You're just really bad at loving yourself. You love yourself with condition and restriction, based on unrealistic demands and impossible standards. You *do* treat others the same way you treat yourself, and that's what I want to address."

And so began my journey into extravagant self-love. This is very different from selfishness. As God explained, it is actually in the best interests of all those around me that I treat myself with compassion. If I walk in extraordinary kindness toward myself, then when I love you the way I love me, I will be expressing God's version of true love, filled with patience, understanding and gentleness.

Maybe you are stuck, too, saying you love yourself, but it doesn't feel true to you. EFT can help you tap into the love and compassion of God. When we receive revelation of how our heavenly Father truly feels about us, we can't help but overflow with that same merciful, gracious, generous love for ourselves and for others.

GOD'S HEART

God cares about our emotional well-being. If we are stressed or overwhelmed in the midst of doing the right things like obeying the Bible and accomplishing ministry work, then what's the big deal. Right?

We find a most compelling verse in the Pentateuch, warning us against just this type of stoic or forced obedience: "Because you did not serve the LORD your God <u>with joy</u> and <u>a glad heart</u>, for the abundance of all things; therefore you shall serve your enemies" (Deuteronomy 28:47–48). Yikes! God is serious about wanting us in a positive emotional space. Here we learn that joy and gladness are at the top of His list.

Holy Spirit began opening Scriptures, showing me again and again that how we feel matters much to our heavenly Father. For example, I learned how laughter is actually a swipe at the enemy. Since satan's strategy is to steal our peace, kill our joy and bring destruction to our spirit, soul and body—wouldn't our laughter be the simplest way to express his total failure? This is why holy laughter is such a distinctive element of revival.

PEACE KEEPERS

I was excited when I found Pastor Bill Johnson of Bethel Church in Redding, California, share a similar idea in his book *Hosting the Presence*.[1]

> He writes: *"It's important to note that violence in the spiritual realm is always a peace-filled moment for His people. That's how the Prince of Peace can crush satan under our feet (Romans 16:20). Another way to put it is every peace-filled moment you experience brings terror to the powers of darkness. Only in the Kingdom of God is peace a military tool."*

Yes! That's exactly what the Lord had been teaching me. He then went on to show me how all throughout the New Testament, holy emotion was a decidedly big player.

Well, I already knew about the fruit of the Spirit—love, joy, and peace (Galatians 5:22). But then Holy Spirit reminded me about the "abiding realities": faith, hope and love. First Corinthians 13 is about having the fruit of the Spirit in our lives or else the gifts don't count. Spiritual gifts such as miracles and prophecy are to demonstrate the spiritual fruit of God's feelings—His patience, kindness and compassion towards us.

What really clinched it for me was when the Lord brought Romans 14:17 onto my radar. Righteousness, peace and joy in the Holy Ghost are actually the very kingdom of God. I'm not sure He could put a higher premium on them than that. And if that wasn't enough, Holy Spirit then showed me how all this divine emotion actually plays a part in our spiritual warfare.

---

1   Johnson, *Hosting the Presence*, 2012.

THE BATTLEGROUND: OUR MINDS AND HEARTS

First, there is the incredibly significant understanding that it is "just" wrong feelings like anger (Ephesians 4:26,27) and unforgiveness that actually give place to the devil in our lives (2 Corinthians 2:10,11). This is why we must not entertain these emotions. This is where the war goes down. We so often think of spiritual warfare as something happening outside of us. But more often than not, it's happening within us.

> *"For though we live in the world, we do not wage war as the world does. The weapons we fight with are not the weapons of the world. On the contrary, they have divine power to demolish strongholds. We demolish arguments and every pretension that sets itself up against the knowledge of God, and we take captive every thought to make it obedient to Christ."* (2 Corinthians 10:3–5)

It is in our minds that the battle is won. We take every thought captive to the obedience of Christ, so we must be vigilant in our thought life. "How long will your wicked thoughts lodge within you?" (Jeremiah 4:14) We don't want to let a thought slip past our awareness unless we want to experience it, because we know that as a man thinks in his heart, so is he (Proverbs 23:7).

We also understand that life and death are in the power of the tongue (Proverbs 18:21). When we declare a thing, it is established (Job 22:28). These Scriptures make it clear we are like our Creator Father in whose image we were made. Just as He did, we create our world with our words (Hebrews 11:3).

However, we need to back it up even further. We need to ensure our thoughts are congruent with our words. But just as important as our thoughts and words aligning with God's thoughts and words, we also must be sure our feelings align with His. This is the place of agreement—spirit, soul and body—and it is a powerful space from which to live.

In our minds we win the spiritual battle by thinking only God's thoughts: whatsoever things are true, honorable, right, pure, lovely, praise-worthy, excellent and virtuous (Philippians 4:8).

In our hearts we win the spiritual battle by feeling only God's emotions: love, joy, peace, faith, hope and compassion (Galatians 5:22). Aligning our thoughts and feelings with God's thoughts and feelings is the most effective supernatural strategy for warfare we have.

Our lives are hidden with Christ in God (Colossians 3:3). When we truly live from that place within Him—inside the mind of Christ, inside the heart of God—we win. We are safe, protected from the enemy, and maintaining the victory Jesus already won for us. When we are living inside Him, we are more than conquerors (Romans 8:37).

KNOWING THE ENEMY

Our enemy is not like God; satan is not omniscient, omnipotent nor omnipresent. We never ascribe these qualities to Gabriel or Michael or any other angel. Why would a fallen angel be any better? The devil is a created being, currently an unemployed cherub, exiled to earth. He was completely disarmed and stripped of all power when Jesus made a public spectacle of him at the cross, triumphing over him (Colossians 2:15).

We know greater is Jesus in us than any enemy in the world (1 John 4:4). God gave all authority to Jesus (Matthew 28:18). Jesus gave it to us (Luke 10:17–19). That means none is left for satan. Jesus rendered the devil entirely useless and voided his power (Hebrews 2:14).

So how does the devil work? How does he sneak in? Since he has been stripped of all authority, how do the forces of darkness have any influence over us?

James 4:7 promises if we resist the devil, he will flee! But let us not forget the first half of that verse: *Submit yourselves to God,* then resist the devil, then he will flee. If we're aware of sin in our hearts and purposefully choose to ignore it, our prayers won't be answered (Psalm 66:18). So what kind of submission to God are we talking about? What kind of sin should we be on guard against that lets satan have his way in our lives?

ENEMY'S ENTRY POINTS

HARBORING ANGER

We re-empower the enemy in our lives when we harbor anger and let it dwell in us. God says not letting go of anger gives the enemy a foothold in our hearts and lives: "Be angry, and yet do not sin; do not let the sun go down on your anger, and do not give the devil an opportunity" (Ephesians 4:26,27).

This is encouraging because here we see anger is not the sin, since we are able to "be angry and sin not" (Ephesians 4:26). Harboring the anger, continually living in the anger and not releasing it to God—that is where momentary, benign anger crosses the line and becomes unhealthy, dangerous, and sinful, allowing the enemy a place in our lives.

Ecclesiastes 7:9 states we must not let anger "lodge" within us, or else we are fools. So while we experience a rush of anger in the heat of the moment, we do not let it live and dwell and abide and get comfortable, taking up residence inside our hearts.

INDULGING IN ANXIETY

Anxiety also lets the enemy influence our lives. Many of us do not consider worry to be a sin. But if we are worrying, then we are not expressing faith in God. And anything not of faith is sin (Romans 14:23). Jesus Himself actually had quite a bit to say about this seemingly inconsequential emotion in Matthew 6:25–34.

> *"Therefore I tell you, do not worry about your life, what you will eat or drink; or about your body, what you will wear. Is not life more than food, and the body more than clothes? Look at the birds of the air; they do not sow or reap or store away in barns, and yet your heavenly Father feeds them. Are you not much more valuable than they?*

> *"Can any one of you by worrying add a single hour to your life? And why do you worry about clothes? See how the flowers of the field grow. They do not labor or spin. Yet I tell you that not even Solomon in all his splendor was dressed like one of these. If that is how God clothes the grass of the field, which is here today and tomorrow is thrown into the fire, will he not much more clothe you—you of little faith?*

> *"So do not worry, saying, 'What shall we eat?' or 'What shall we drink?' or 'What shall we wear?' For the pagans run after all these things, and your heavenly Father knows that you need them. But seek first his kingdom and his righteousness, and all these things will be given to you as well. Therefore do not worry about tomorrow, for tomorrow will worry about itself. Each day has enough trouble of its own."*

Worry is not as harmless as the enemy would lead us to believe. When we allow ourselves to entertain anxious thoughts and feelings, we are basically saying, "God, I don't believe that You will provide for me. I don't believe You will take care of me." We are telling God we don't trust Him. And without faith it is impossible to please Him (Hebrews 11:6). Understand whatever we ponder in our hearts, mull over in our minds and talk much about, we create and make true in our lives.

ENTERTAINING FEAR

We also re-empower our adversary through our fear (Hebrews 2:15). This is a big entry point for the enemy! We need to recognize fear is faith in reverse; fear is faith in satan.

Our faith is incredibly strong! We move mountains with it (Matthew 17:20). Therefore, we are responsible to pay close attention to how we wield such a mighty weapon by carefully considering where we place our faith. We must not have more faith in the power of the devil to destroy us than we have faith in the power of our heavenly Father to protect, provide and care for us.

Job said, "What I feared has come upon me; what I dreaded has happened to me" (Job 3:25). He was expecting the worst, and according to his faith, it was done unto him (Matthew 9:29). His story is an example to us that makes it crystal clear why we never want to indulge ungodly fear in our hearts or in our minds. Ever.

WITHHOLDING FORGIVENESS

We dangerously and inadvertently re-empower the enemy when we walk in unforgiveness. The Bible warns we create a space in our lives for the devil to dwell when we entertain unforgiveness in our hearts.

> *"But one whom you forgive anything, I forgive also; for indeed what I have forgiven, if I have forgiven anything, I did it for your sakes in the presence of Christ, so that no advantage would be taken of us by satan, for we are not ignorant of his schemes."* (2 Corinthians 2:10,11)

Revelation 12:10 calls satan the "accuser of the brethren" and he constantly accuses others to us. He lies and twists truth. He pushes us to see others through his lens of distortion, tempting us to walk in bitterness, judgment and resentment.

In the sixth chapter of Matthew, we find the Lord teaching His disciples how to pray. Jesus then makes a very direct, unmistakable declaration: "For if you forgive other people when they sin against you, your heavenly Father will also forgive you. **But if you do not forgive others their sins, your Father will not forgive your sins**" (Matthew 6:14–15).

Clearly, walking in unforgiveness is not an option for Christians. This is more than enough reason to forgive everyone of everything at all times. A few chapters later in Matthew 18, however, Jesus underscores His teaching when He shares the parable of the unforgiving servant. The indebted servant is forgiven his enormous debt but instead of being grateful, he turns around and demands payment from his fellow slave who owes him a much lesser amount.

The servant's master is moved with anger over this injustice and has the unforgiving servant turned over to the tormenters to be tortured. Jesus teaches we must extend mercy and forgive one another from our heart; otherwise, we too will experience torment (Matthew 18:21–35). Withholding mercy, compassion and forgiveness allows the enemy to take advantage of us and opens the door to all manner of pain.

ACCEPTING FALSE GUILT

One last enemy entry point into our lives is false guilt. Essentially, guilt is what we feel when we don't forgive ourselves, so it's closely related to unforgiveness. As Christians we are often much better at forgiving our family, friends and even our enemies than we are at forgiving ourselves.

False guilt is when we confess and repent but still feel bad about our transgression. Once we repent of a sin, God no longer remembers it (Hebrews 10:17). As far as the east is from the west, so far has He removed those transgressions from us (Psalm 103:12).

Again, it is the accuser of the brethren who heaps condemnation upon us and makes us feel guilty about things God has chosen to forget. We must learn to be more like our heavenly Father and develop a case of holy amnesia!

Apostle Paul reminds us there is therefore now *no condemnation* for those who are in Christ Jesus (Romans 8:1). We must not denigrate Jesus' sacrificial death by presuming our sin is more powerful than His cleansing blood. It is finished! Let go of false guilt and be set free from condemnation. Hallelujah!

WHAT EFT DOES BEST

So why are we having this conversation in a book on Emotional Freedom Techniques? Because everything we are discussing boils down to emotions: anger, worry, fear, unforgiveness, and guilt. Emotions are what EFT handles best.

This book devotes entire chapters on how to apply tapping to worry and to unforgiveness, demonstrating in practical terms how to deal with these ungodly emotions. EFT can enable us to neutralize our negative feelings and connect with God's emotions of love, peace, joy, freedom and fearlessness.

We may believe that our emotions are not a big deal; that having the right feelings is a small thing. That is a lie from the enemy foisted on the Church to keep Her from living into the strong, healed, glory-filled destiny God has purposed for His Bride from the very beginning.

Now is the time for us to step into that place of victorious peace and overflowing joy. In fact, these heavenly feelings are actually what protect us in our spiritual battles and cause us to always triumph in Christ (2 Corinthians 2:14).

SPIRITUAL ARMOR

We prepare for our spiritual battle with a breastplate of *faith and love,* and a helmet of *hope* (1 Thessalonians 5:8). Not to mention feet shod in *peace* (Ephesians 6:15).

Much like the enemy's entry points are negative emotions, the converse is also true. Positive, godly emotions keep us safe from harm. Love is the piece of armor which covers our hearts. Hope is the helmet which defends our minds. Peace is what shields our feet.

From head to toe we are clothed in holy emotion and that is what protects us. Indeed, we know it is the *peace* of God that guards our hearts and minds (Philippians 4:7).

Feelings that guard us? Emotions that protect us? What an amazing revelation!

SCIENCE AGREES

Scientific studies confirm our feelings and emotions are important to our mind-body wellness. "Recent estimates indicate as many as 90 percent of the people seeking medical care are doing so because of a stress-related disorder."[2] Stress is an emotion. It is the opposite of being in peace and joy.

---

2   Dispenza, *Evolve Your Brain*, 275.

Scripture discusses this mind-body correlation of health in 3 John 2: "Beloved, I pray that in all respects you may prosper and be in good health, just as your soul prospers." Not only does God want us to be emotionally healthy, He explains how living in His holy feelings also makes us physically healthy.

To the degree that our soul prospers, our physical health prospers. They are connected and one affects the other. It is very difficult to experience health in our body if we are broken emotionally or spiritually. Our body is an outer reflection and expression of the inner health of our soul.

The more we practice EFT, the more we are able to get our emotional and spiritual brokenness healed. As a result, the health of our physical body naturally follows suit.

FEARLESS FREEDOM AND A GRATEFUL HEART

What are some other positive emotions we can expect to experience through tapping? Freedom is an awesome one. It was for freedom that Christ set us free (Galatians 5:1). Therefore, we are already free. But just like the slave who didn't act after the ratification of the Thirteenth Amendment set in motion by the Emancipation Proclamation, we, too, can choose to stay in bondage to debilitating fears and paralyzing emotions. Christ has already won our freedom at the cross. Now He is providing EFT as one of His many "gifts of healings" for us to live into that freedom. Let us avail ourselves of the gift.

God is good all the time, and He is in a good mood. We want to please God and live in faith that these things are true (Hebrews 11:6). A tangible way we demonstrate our faith and trust in Him and His goodness is through thanksgiving. We know we are to enter God's presence with thanksgiving, but it's easy to think giving thanks is something we do—an action.

However, before it is something we do, it is something we feel. We feel thankful. We feel appreciation. We feel gratitude. Then as an expression of that inward emotion, we give thanks outwardly and verbally to demonstrate our grateful inner state of being.

Gratitude is a good space in which to dwell. Right up there with compassion, it is one of the most powerful emotions we can live in. When we're grateful, we are expressing faith we have already received what we have asked for. This kind of grateful faith is a supernatural magnet that draws to us that for which we are thankful.

We no longer worry about the future, but instead live as if our prayers have already been answered (Mark 11:22–24). In the eternal now of God, where no linear timeline exists, we *have* already received from Him all we have requested (1 John 5:14–15). God gave us everything when He gave us Jesus. It has already been done. And that is definitely something to be excited, grateful, and happy about!

SOUNDS OF LAUGHTER

The sound of joyful shouting and salvation is in the dwelling of the godly (Psalm 118:15). Pastor Bill Johnson was right: "Our peace-filled moments do bring terror to the enemy." And what is the best outward expression of peace? Laughter! In a kingdom of joy, what is the official language spoken? Laughter! In God's presence is fullness of joy and a joyful heart is good medicine (Psalm 16:11; Proverbs 17:22). Well, what do joyful hearts and fullness of joy sound like? Yes, laughter!

One of my favorite descriptions of God and how He interacts with His children is in the book of Zechariah: *"The Lord your God is in your midst, the Mighty One, will save you. He will rejoice over you with gladness, He will quiet you in His love, He will rejoice over you with singing"* (Zechariah 3:17). It's a beautiful picture of a Father so pleased and proud of His beloved sons and daughters. His glad heart is so full of delight in us, it overflows with joyful song!

When we see Jesus as He is, we become like Him (1 John 3:2). According to Psalm 2:4, He is sitting in heaven laughing! When our eyes are fixed on Him and our hearts set on things above, we are able to relax, too. We can be still, let go and laugh as well, knowing *He is God,* and that's all that truly matters (Psalm 46:10). He is our Shepherd, and that's all we want. No matter what is happening in this natural world, we're living to a different Kingdom. And EFT can allow us to live out of it effortlessly.

ABOVE ALL ELSE

We know that above all else, we must guard our heart, for everything we do flows from it (Proverbs 4:23). EFT equips us to fulfill this Scripture. Through tapping, we can guard our heart. Through tapping, we can connect with the feelings of God's Spirit. Through tapping, we can let go of toxic emotions.

Academically, we know we should let these things go. But practically, how do we do that? Tapping is the *how* in how we let anger go. How we let bitterness and unforgiveness go. How we let fear, anxiety and sadness go. It's not something we do; it's something we release. EFT empowers us to release this negativity by moving it out of our cellular memory, out of our hearts, and out of our minds—for good.

STUDIES, STATISTICS AND SURVIVOR STORIES

Dr. Joseph Mercola has built the most visited natural health website in the world, reaching 25 million readers each month. He is a Christian who sees tapping as a gift from God and teaches "EFT is done through you, not by you." On his training DVDs, Dr. Mercola describes the immediate and powerful results he witnesses from tapping as "therapy at the speed of light."[3] Following are a small sampling of the ground-breaking studies illustrating the extraordinary benefits of tapping:

"A randomized, controlled trial of veterans who received EFT found that their pain dropped by 41%, even though they were being treated for PTSD, not for pain.[4] The reductions in pain were simply a fortunate side effect of their PTSD treatment."

"A case study also found EFT to be effective for dyslexia (McCallion, 2012), and another for TBI or traumatic brain injury (Craig, Bach, Groesbeck, & Benor, 2009). One randomized controlled trial found reductions in TBI symptoms of 41% after six sessions of EFT for PTSD (Church & Palmer-Hoffman, 2013). Dr. Paul Swingle (2011) found EFT useful in the treatment of seizure disorders. There are also many accounts on EFTUniverse.com of people who've used EFT for diabetes."[5]

"Research performed by the Iraq Vets Stress Project also demonstrates the effectiveness of EFT. In a study that included 100 veterans with severe PTSD, 90 percent of the veterans had such a reduction in symptoms that they no longer met the clinical criteria for PTSD after six one-hour EFT sessions! Sixty percent no longer met PTSD criteria after just three EFT sessions. At the three-month follow-up, the gains remained stable, suggesting lasting and potentially permanent resolution of the problem."[6]

A quote directly from the project website[7] states: "After 3 EFT sessions 40% of the sample (both groups) still met the clinical criteria for PTSD. This decreased to 14% after 6 sessions and remained stable at the 3-month follow-up. Conclusions: EFT resolved PTSD in 86% of treated patients."

---

3   Dr. Joseph Mercola's Emotional Freedom Techniques, Disc 1, Introduction.
4   Church, *The Genie in Your Genes*, 244.
5   www.eomega.org/article/tap-your-way-to-healing-ptsd-with-eft
6   articles.mercola.com/sites/articles/archive/2013/12/26/emotional-freedom-technique.aspx
7   www.stressproject.org/documents/poster%20for%20usuhs.pdf

EFT work has also proven effective with genocide survivors in Rwanda. Now adults, these orphans experienced incredible healing. A documentary reports "trauma outbreaks were reduced by an astonishing 90% in just one year."[8]

Even the American Psychological Association (APA) is on board and members now formally recognize the indisputable benefits of tapping. In a critical review published in its journal *Review of General Psychology,* researchers found that EFT "consistently demonstrated strong effect sizes and other positive statistical results that far exceed chance after relatively few treatment sessions."[9]

Although no guarantees can be made by any EFT Practitioner or EFT book, the mountain of research continues to grow with near-miraculous accounts of life-changing breakthrough. EFT has been consistently demonstrated to be an effective approach with trauma victims and soldiers returning from war.[10] Counselors have used tapping with school-shooting survivors in the U.S. and displaced refugees overseas. There is almost always one thing in common[11]: they not only achieve outstanding results, but also the stressful consequences are neutralized and positive benefits realized more quickly than anyone expects.

DANCING IN THE RAIN

We will also share stories in this book of how tapping can help with our everyday events and letting go of frustration and disappointment, reducing stress emotionally and physically, and overcoming panic and overwhelm. EFT can be used to address the big issues, the small issues, and everything in between.

Of course, we know this world has its trials and trouble, but Jesus said to be encouraged because He has overcome the world (John 16:33). While it is true we were never promised a life without rain, we can certainly choose to live like Jesus and have peace in the midst of the storms (Mark 4:39).

Tapping can unlock the peace within us. It opens us to experience the Kingdom of Heaven that is within (Luke 17:21). It unblocks the energy and life of the Spirit to flow freely through us—spirit, soul and body.

---

8   You can watch a moving eight-minute story on this incredible outreach at www. youtube.com/watch?v=3JLugqjn3o8
9   *Review of General Psychology* December 2012: 16(4); 364-380
10   www.eomega.org/article/tap-your-way-to-healing-ptsd-with-eft
11   www.innersource.net/ep/images/stories/downloads/EP_DisasterRelief.pdf

REDEMPTION: TAKING BACK WHAT THE ENEMY STOLE

In closing out our introduction to EFT, Sherrie and I want to make one point abundantly clear. We do not want to give up any more ground to satan. God wants to restore what the enemy has taken from us. What do we mean by that?

God created energy. Individuals of various faiths and beliefs have explored energy psychology in general, and EFT specifically, and many have benefited greatly from their practice. Energy psychology is simply a mind-body approach to understanding and improving our lives. It focuses on the relationship between bio-energy systems, neuro- and electro-physiological processes, and how our thoughts and emotions play a role in our health.[12]

God created our neurological and bio-chemical systems to work in an integrated, holistic fashion, and He created our bodies to respond to epigenetics, the power of right thinking and feeling. It's how *the Lord* designed us to be.

God created us in His image, and He is Spirit (John 4:24). So living into the supernatural world of spirit and energy is His original plan and intention for us. The fact that someone who is not a Christian practices EFT does not in any way affect us or influence our decision to enjoy this blessing from God as Bible-believing, Spirit-filled Christians. Tapping is a precious gift from our heavenly Father to us, and it is high time we unwrap it!

DO YOU WANT TO BE WELL?

Jesus asked the invalid at the Pool of Bethesda, "Do you want to be well?" From someone who has suffered for 38 years, the answer would seem obvious; however, the man made excuses for why he couldn't get better. But Jesus offered a solution (John 5:5–8).

While God is certainly in the instantaneous supernatural healing ministry now as much as ever, sometimes, we have a part to play in miracles. Peter first had to climb out of the boat and put his own feet down, one in front of the other. Only after he did something natural, did Peter experience something supernatural as he walked on water (Matthew 14:25–29). God did His part, but first Peter had to do his. And it looked crazy!

---

12 Church, *The Genie in Your Genes*, 153, 163–165.

Peter didn't care how he looked because He wanted to get closer to Jesus. He wanted to know God's power and experience more than he had known before. In a lot of ways, like Peter, we're in the same boat! The question we need to ask is what part do we play in the unfolding of our miracle? From which boat do we have to climb out? Beyond what limited box or belief do we need to get? What new thing do we need to try?

GIFTS OF HEALINGS

*"God has appointed in the church...**miracles**, then **gifts of healings**..."*
(1 Corinthians 12:28)

While we all desire and prefer the immediate miracle, we can be encouraged by the many other ways God also heals us. The Bible states that in addition to miracles, God also provides us "gifts of healings," and both "gifts" and "healings" are plural in the Greek. This is good news because it means we have a multiplicity of ways in which God can and will heal us.

He is Jehovah Raphe, the Lord Who Heals (Exodus 15:26). Healing, therefore, is not simply what God does, it is also Who He is! Healing is in His DNA, and He loves to see His children walk in glorious health. First Corinthians 12:28 makes it clear God has made various gifts of healings available to us, which we can appropriate and live into.

EFT is one of those gifts.

Charity Kayembe

SECTION ONE: EFT—
Emotional Freedom Techniques

SUB-SECTION ONE:
EFT Explained

CHAPTER 1

What is EFT?

Emotional Freedom Techniques (EFT) is an amazing self-help tool used to repair the damage we cause ourselves by learning to de-program earlier learned bad behaviors by eliminating the negative thoughts and beliefs of our past. The process is based on fairly new neuroscience research that shows how emotional trauma contributes directly to many, if not all, diseases. This research shows that "tapping" reduces the emotional charge around our negatively impactful memories and events that still trigger our emotional distress today, even though the incidents may have happened decades ago.

Tapping—using our fingertips to tap on face and body acupuncture points—combined with elements of Cognitive and Exposure Therapies, signal to part of our brain (the amygdala) that we are now safe, in the present, and that the event that still triggers us into unhealthy thoughts and behaviors is truly in the past. (See Chapter 5, for pressure points photos and a tapping instructions overview.)

You see, our subconscious mind does not differentiate between our past and present. Scripture supports this concept when it states in 2 Peter 3:8b, "With the Lord a day is like a thousand years, and a thousand years are like a day." Because of the mingling of the past and present, we have subconscious access to only about 3–5% of what our mind is doing in the background of our life.

BEAUTIFUL BRAIN

Dr. Caroline Leaf writes, "At any moment, your brain is creatively performing about 400 billion actions, of which you are only conscious of about 2,000."[13] As a Christian cognitive neuroscientist, Dr. Leaf is telling us that most of what we

---

13 Leaf, *Who Switched Off My Brain*, 3.

think on a second by second basis doesn't even register in our "thinking" mind. Most of what goes on with each of us on a daily basis is hidden behind a shroud of tangled nerve cells, feelings, and distant emotions we often work hard to keep in check, as we overlook what our body and mind are trying to tell us about our health, environment, and our relationships with each other.

EFT allows us to go deeper within ourselves, our actions, and behaviors to not only understand why we do the things we do (much of it to one another!), but also to repair the damage these subconscious thoughts and feelings do to us, since they contribute to cancer, heart disease, auto-immune problems, strokes, diabetes, hypothyroidism, obesity, and other rampant modern diseases.

Dr. Caroline Leaf continues, "Research shows that around 87% of illnesses can be attributed to our thought life, and approximately 13% to diet, genetics, and environment. Studies conclusively link more chronic diseases (also known as lifestyle diseases) to an epidemic of toxic emotions in our culture."[14]

Dr. Leaf quotes Dr. Bruce Lipton to say that 98% of all diseases are lifestyle choices, or as she interprets that statistic to say, it's all about our thinking.[15]

In some ways, this is very good news for us! We now know all our negative buried thoughts and feelings are doing more damage to us than eating too much and exercising too little! However, we still need to eat our vegetables and fruits and walk an hour a day. More importantly, we must control the negativity running amok in the background of our minds.

Few of these thoughts are godly thoughts. If they were godly, then they wouldn't be causing all health issues we face. What kinds of thoughts are they? Thoughts that include anger, disgust, resentment, grief, fear, and anxiety about all types of situations and people in our lives. We love to mull over who did what to us when. We are human. That is what we do.

But God tells us He has a better way. We are to love one another as He loved us (John 13:34). We all desire to do just that, but we are also like Apostle Paul in Romans 7:15, "I do not understand what I do. For what I want to do I do not do, but what I hate I do."

---

14 Ibid., 5.
15 Ibid., 37.

The St. Joseph Baltimore catechism taught me as a child to love God and to serve Him. I personally want to do this, as I am sure you do, too, but I often fail God miserably in this desire.

Why does that happen this way? Why can we not change our thought patterns to conform to the godly ones we desire?

Neuroscience research has now answered these questions, and it's all wrapped up in the chemicals coursing through our body. These include hormones, neurotransmitters, and peptides, along with an amazing array of micronutrients we eat everyday, hopefully, from that well-balanced diet our moms taught us to eat when she placed veggies and fruits on our plate.

As these chemicals come and go within our bodies—based on environmental occurrences outside and inside the body—they leave a lasting imprint on the mind, which scientists now understand to be our entire bodies. Yes, you heard me! Your mind is really your body.

EFT is a self-help tool, but it does have variations and uses. Simply put, the more complicated or involved one's trauma is the more one needs to understand the techniques in order to get more complete tapping results.

RESOURCES FOR PEOPLE NEW TO EFT

For those who are new to using EFT, try using the basic instructions that follow. If you find you need further assistance in learning more advanced techniques, I suggest three things:

First, consider purchasing a copy of Sherrie's original book—*EFT for Christians*—from Sherrie's website, EFTforChristians.com. This book contains a more detailed and fuller manual on tapping.

Second, attend an EFT class to gain hands-on experience and fine-tune your techniques with a live instructor. A class can enable you to continue learning and growing your own personal tapping work. You may contact Sherrie at EFTforChristians@gmail.com for more information.

Third, hire a Christian EFT Practitioner to assist you in clearing more of your issues and trauma. Life experiences, trauma, and the degree of their impact on our lives vary from person to person. A Christian EFT Practitioner can be a valuable resource to help you get unstuck, go deeper, and clear out more of your issues.

In addition to the tapping instructions overview in Chapter 5 of this book, please refer also to the following manual, guide and video resources available online:

Charity Kayembe assisted her father Dr. Mark Virkler in creating some simple how-to tapping instructions that may be freely downloaded from her website: www.GloryWaves.org/EFT

A multiple-page document outlining amazing research articles that explain how God made our mind-body to work can be downloaded from the resource page on EFTforChristians.com.

To subscribe to Sherrie's EFT for Christians blog, go to: http://eftfor christian.blogspot.com/

For a few EFT videos with Sherrie tapping with a client, go to: www. youtube.com/channel/UCmxsHG9CFSWot3rDZac2rSw/videos

To join our Facebook page, EFT for Christians Discussion Group, please visit www.facebook.com/groups/352652964926202/

To view study materials or for more information on EFT with Sherrie Rice Smith, please visit www.facebook.com/groups/307887129394873/

CHAPTER 2

EFT in Action

When a negative, fear-ridden and anxiety-producing event happens to you, it registers within the structures of your brain. When your brain decides it needs to record this event as a good life lesson, it imprints the memory somewhere in your body. It can choose your liver, your heart, your left knee, your lower back—anywhere. The mind chooses the spot, and you discover that spot 5, 10, 20, or 30 years later when that body part begins to break down and cause you pain or when you receive other diagnostic news from your physician. Let me illustrate how this process unfolds and how Emotional Freedom Techniques jumps into action.

THE GREEN PICK-UP TRUCK

Let's imagine you were involved in a traffic accident at the age of 5. The driver of a green pick-up truck lost control and smashed into the passenger side of the beige sedan your mom was driving. Your mom wasn't hurt, but you suffered a badly broken right arm, necessitating surgery that resulted in a heavy plaster cast for 7 weeks in July—the first month of your summer vacation from school.

The family planned a one-week-long vacation at a sandy beach with lots of summer fun on the docket with all of your cousins who you rarely see because they live 200 miles away. You had been excited for this summer vacation since Christmas when your mom and dad planned it. The accident ruined your vacation, since all you could do was to sit on the sidelines watching all the fun from a distance. All the adults tried to cheer you up, but nothing made you feel any better. You do your 5-year-old's best to hold it together in your own way, so you don't ruin everyone else's vacation. But you thereafter remember being just plain miserable inside.

Here you are today, an adult of 42 years, and you suddenly develop a huge case of anxiety. It appeared out of the blue, and nothing you do can seem to bring it under control. You even visited your doctor, who prescribes an anti-anxiety drug, but even that doesn't seem to lessen this horrible feeling.

You struggle for months on end, missing several days of work when it's impossible to get out of bed to greet the day. You are at your wits end when a friend suggests you call a local EFT practitioner. Stumped about the cause of this debilitating nervous feeling, you'll agree to just about anything.

As the EFT practitioner taps with you about your present-day nervousness that seems to be trapping you, you suddenly remember this traffic accident 37 years ago. You've not thought about it since that messed up non-vacation at the beach with your cousins.

The practitioner has you tune into all the sensory information around that accident three decades ago, and you begin to wonder what in the world does this event have to do with your present-day anxiety.

Holy Spirit is joined to your spirit, so as you tap into your subconscious, you are accessing His flow of wisdom deep within you (1 Corinthians 6:17; John 7:37–39). If this vacation debacle is the event your spirit brings up for you to tap about, then it is calling your attention to that car wreck! Based on the process of EFT, let me explain how this tapping session may unfold.

FINDING THE TRIGGER

The color green has surfaced as a detail of your accident. As you tune into a specific color of green, you realize it is the same exact color green that out-of-control pick-up truck was painted long ago. It was an odd lively color of 1980s green, one that was in vogue back in that decade. You tap down the anxiety associated with that green color with your EFT practitioner, leaving you feeling fairly calm in the moment. You then suddenly realize your boss recently repainted your office with this vibrant green color. That, too, is the *exact* same retro shade of green the pick-up truck was painted that ruined your summer vacation when you were 5 years old!

Your EFT practitioner smiles, while assisting you to tap away the connection between the danger of the green pick-up truck and the now dangerous green-painted walls of your refurbished office!

What was that all about, you ask? That green wall paint is what we call a "trigger." A trigger is a sight, sound, or smell, anything sensory that takes you back to a negative memory of an earlier time. You don't experience the memory as something in the past; you experience the memory as if it happened today with all the physical feelings and subconscious thoughts of when it happened 37 years before. Triggers bring the past harmful event back into our subconscious minds in full living color with intense emotion, just as if it were still happening right here, right now.[16]

These memories are often so subtle we don't recognize what is going on inside of us until we use a process like EFT to allow us to associate in our conscious mind what went on in the past and how it is affecting us today in the present.

Once your EFT practitioner helps tap down the associated memory from this green paint trigger, your nervousness can dissipate. It dissipates because your mind now understands via the actual tapping that the green painted walls are not dangerous and the green walls are not the pick-up truck uncontrollably flying down the highway ready to smash into your mom's car with you inside!

Are all tapping cases this easily dispelled and neutralized? No, sadly not. Many of them can be highly complicated, involving various intense, intertwined memories and events along with countless internal chemicals and numerous sensory receptors.

We EFT practitioners tap with clients, helping them learn how to do EFT for themselves, but as with much in life, there are variables to the process, and no guarantees as to the success in any one given case or session.

We now understand the more intense the adrenaline and cortisol reactions during a stressful event, the more likely the mind will encode the memory long-term. Auto accidents, hospitalizations, abuse, weather disasters, death, divorce, job losses, mental illnesses, alcohol use, drug use, and so many others tend to be intense familial and environmental incidents that we remember, and so do our bodies because our mind stores every detail within the cells of our body.

---

16   Van der Kolk, *The Body Keeps the Score*, 66–67.

Dr. Caroline Leaf has thoughts on this idea, too: "Toxic thought and emotions disrupt homeostasis and cause structural changes down to the cellular level."[17]

The fictitious 5-year-old you in this short vignette could have just as well presented back pain, arm pain, or any other kind of pain. Our mind will eventually transfer our emotional pain into something we understand—physical pain.

Dr. Leaf explains it this way: "Suppressed emotional pain doesn't just disappear. It can turn into lingering physical pain."[18] And to this I add that emotional pain can also turn into physical disease, and it very often does.

Triggers from early incidents in our lives are physical and emotional stress. That stress lives on long after the event is over and everyone has forgotten about it. Everyone, that is, except you and your "bodymind," a term coined by Dianne Connelly.[19] Stress literally eats away at your body's organs because your subconscious mind runs 97% of your life[20] and there is little you can do about it until you consider applying the balm of God's EFT, or possibly another modality, to your internal emotional wounds.

17 Leaf, *Who Switched Off My Brain*, page 57.
18 Ibid., 77.
19 Pert, *Molecules of Emotion*, page 187.
20 Lipton, *The Biology of Belief*, 2008, 33.

SUB-SECTION TWO:
The Science Behind EFT

CHAPTER 3

What is Stress?

Stress is an *internal* response to pressures, worries, or stimuli that causes a disruption in our internal stability (homeostasis), producing physiological symptoms and hardship on our internal organs.[21]

Stress can be physical, mental, emotional, or spiritual. Stress can be acute, occasional, or chronic. The first two types of stress come and go depending on situations. The human body can cope well with short-term stress. It was made to do that in order to keep us physically safe. Chronic stress that goes on for over a year or for decades is the problematic type. It never seems to cease, grinding away at our organs, causing long-term damage, like hypertension or worse.[22]

Stressors are ones we create or they can be ones foisted on us by others. Making poor life choices causes stress. Exercise is great; sitting in a chair is bad. Most of us know what is good for us and what isn't. Vegetables are good; potato chips are not. Good sleep is terrific for our health; late nights drinking with friends is not.

Often, these choices are sinful habits or poorly chosen life actions that sadden God, but He sits back and allows us to do as we wish. We have free will to do as we want—follow His commands or do life our own way. Other times, stressors are caused by sinful choices other people make that directly or indirectly affect us. These are the consequences of sin.

For some people, physiology is stiff, hard science, maybe even a bit boring, so allow me to weave in a client's story with the scientific mechanism of how stress

---

21 Mate, *When the Body Says NO*, 34.
22 Church, *The Genie in Your Genes*, 253–254.

affects us and how God also created another way out of "the stress mess," so to speak, via tapping. God's creative powers are so amazing! The intricacy of how our Father made us in all its depth and beauty is mind-boggling.

"WHITE COAT SYNDROME"

AgnesMary who is nearing her seventh decade of life, requested my tapping services to deal with anxiety around her upcoming doctor's appointments. It sounded like a simple set of tapping sessions, but I'm experienced enough to know that "the problem is never the problem," as we say in the tapping field.

For some time now, upon visiting a physician's office, AgnesMary found her vital signs skyrocketing, something known as "White Coat Syndrome," or a variation of it. This concerned her deeply, and rightly so, because the doctor was pushing medication as the solution to the problem. AgnesMary desperately wanted to avoid more meds.

As we practitioners always do when tapping with clients, we start with what the client presents (i.e., their complaint and reason for coming) before delving into the heavier, underlying problems. I have clients begin tapping immediately at the start of the appointment because this begins to "soften up" the subconscious to let go of what truly is happening deep down within the inner mind, revealing the true heart of the actual issue Holy Spirit wants us to tap on. After praying to open the tapping session, I queried AgnesMary on her doctor's office anxiety.

AgnesMary seemed to carry most of her bodily sensations in her head—heaviness, buzzing, and pressure, accompanied by a little pain here and there. I confirmed her doctor had examined her head for these symptoms to make sure something more serious wasn't going on. Her reply was, "He says there is nothing wrong with my head, but if I don't get my blood pressure down, there will be!"

Researchers have shown that strong negative emotions stress our bodies, even when little or no symptoms show up physically; the damage has probably already begun. Occasionally, certain blood tests may give us an indication of where a disease may show up later in life.[23]

As AgnesMary and I prayed and tapped, we asked God to release the symptoms and what they represented, and AgnesMary began to open up more.

---

23 Ibid., 129.

Her father had been a strict, literal Bible-believing Christian who saw little reason to enjoy much in life. Everything was, "his way or the highway," AgnesMary related to me. She remembered feeling like she was walking on eggshells much of her childhood, which now as an adult, left her with some ambiguous feelings about God and who He was.

While her thinking told her Jesus died for her sins on the cross, she still didn't know if she was good enough to go to heaven. "What happens if I die in my sleep and I haven't confessed all my sins before bed?" she asked me. I asked her if she was "saved." AgnesMary answered she had given her heart to Jesus at a young age of 8. "You are saved and you have a place in heaven," I reassured her, but still I knew she doubted me, as they were just words to her. Something else was underpinning this belief pattern. I prayed that God through tapping would reveal what was underneath her belief here.

She continued telling me how rebellious she felt in spite of spending so much time reading Scripture. She felt doubt and fear burning a hole in her heart. We tapped on both of those feelings, which were a 5 on the SUD scale (see Chapter 5 for a full explanation of this scale, if you aren't already familiar with it), and they quickly dropped down to a 0. "I know my sins are covered by Jesus. I guess I just have to believe that, but it seems hard to do," she told me.

At this point AgnesMary returned to memories about her Papa. She had now begun feeling some sympathy for him because she had a vague feeling her Papa's parents were rough on him as a youngster.

EARLY MEMORIES

We tapped on an early memory of her dad threatening her while he was under the influence of alcohol. He was going to ram the car he was driving, with AgnesMary in the front seat beside him, into a big tree down an old dirt lane "to put us both out of our misery."

Obviously, a lot of fear was bound up in this memory that neutralized nicely from an 8 SUDS to a 1 SUDS, with about four rounds of tapping. Mixed in with the fear was quite a bit of anger at her father for doing such a thing to an innocent 6-year-old child. The anger, which had a 6 SUDS, melted away with the fear. "Dad was doing the best he could," AgnesMary said.

We tapped on other memories of her father berating her when she did anything good in school or when she wanted to dress up for a class dance. He'd ask her,

"Who do you think you are?" She seemed to understand he felt "tortured" about not being good enough, and she felt she inherited that trait from him.

According to today's field of Epigenetics, in an environmental sense, AgnesMary did inherit this "I'm not good enough" trait from him—she learned how to carry her emotions the way her father most likely did. Children learn many things from their parents (as we'll learn in chapter 16), including how to handle emotions and life events, and these lessons will later determine their own genetic disposition of what and when diseases develop.[24]

AgnesMary jumped to another memory of an older brother possibly sexually molesting her, but she dropped that topic quickly. She segued into other memories of her dad and how he always required a completely quiet house when he arrived home from work. When she was a teenager, he would never allow her to go out in the evenings with friends. Work around the house was all her dad knew, and it was what he expected from the rest of the family, too.

After tapping for several sessions, AgnesMary reported back to me that her anxiety did subside somewhat, but her blood pressure had only dropped a few points, not quite enough to satisfy her doctor.

Knowing what I now know about tapping, had AgnesMary tapped another few sessions, we could have neutralized additional events associated with living with an alcoholic father and the briefly mentioned sexual assault by her brother, possibly helping her anxiety level to diminish even further. AgnesMary chose not to continue our tapping sessions; however, she was determined to tap alone.

As many EFT practitioners do, I gave AgnesMary "homework" between sessions. Because so many things in her life were causing her anxiety, and I only outlined a few here, she needed to salve her central nervous system with some EFT balm, helping to slow down her overactive stress system. Sadly, AgnesMary never complied with my request to tap daily. "I don't know if I want to heal. Maybe I should just focus on God," she told me near the end of our sessions together.

Just like AgnesMary, we all feel stress, something within our body simply doesn't feel right. Dr. Peter Levine calls this a "felt sense."[25] In AgnesMary's case, the

---

24 For a simple videotaped explanation of epigenetics, please see www.youtube. com/watch?v=JvW4XAu_dt8
25 Levine, *In An Unspoken Voice*, 150.

elevating of her blood pressure every time she entered a clinic or hospital setting informed her that something buried deep within was bothering her.

Recently, the American Psychological Association commissioned a stress study two years in a row and found that approximately 25% of Americans are experiencing high levels of stress (8 or more on a 10-point scale), while another 50% report moderately high levels of stress (4 to 7 on the same scale). Those numbers leave about 30% of us experiencing a less stressful existence! It appears modern life leaves all of us fairly stressed out.

There are many articles outlining how stress is going to make us ill, and worse yet, be the cause of our demise! This is precisely why learning EFT can be an effective skill to counterbalance all this pressure and trauma.

AgnesMary had multiple memories of her childhood, and few of them were pleasant. Her father was a strict man, who certainly appeared to have doubts about God and life, causing him to be what seemed like a joyless, dour person who expected the same thought processes from his children. AgnesMary was an apt pupil.

There are reasons we do what we do, by choice or not, and tapping can often undo those beliefs and ideas, most of which we've had since childhood. We aren't held hostage to our choices or the choices of others, but it is our responsibility to change what we can in life for the better. Remaining a "victim" to the whims of others no longer holds water with EFT coming to the mainstream! AgnesMary understood that EFT could help relieve her symptoms. She made the phone call.

FIGHT, FLIGHT OR FREEZE

When stress hits us out of the blue, it immediately activates a physiological response called Fight, Flight or Freeze (FFF). This reaction prepares us for an emergency. You don't choose FFF, the response just happens chemically inside you. Body changes begin before you may even notice there is a problem. The autonomic nervous system (ANS) kicks in. The ANS is the *automatic* part of your neurology, and it has two branches: the sympathetic (SNS) and parasympathetic (PNS).[26]

The ANS is responsible for your heart beating, your lungs breathing, your food digesting, your cortisol and blood sugar rising, your hand moving toward that

---

26   Van der Kolk, *The Body Keeps the Score*, 77.

cup of coffee before you even think of picking up the cup. (That actually happens. The next time you are reading a book while drinking a beverage, watch how often you reach for the cup before you "think" of reaching for it! There is a nano-second delay between the action and the thought, with the action coming first.)[27]

In stress, your body does the same thing. God put in you a mechanism where your subconscious mind senses danger before your conscious mind even realizes something is wrong, giving you that split-second of extra time to move out of the way of the oncoming threat.

During short-term stress—like right after the automobile that headed directly at you veers out of your way—the physiological symptoms of your body's reaction dissipate fairly quickly. The problem with stress isn't the short-term shots of adrenaline, norepinephrine, and cortisol that are immediately secreted and quickly returned to normal levels, but the chronic elevation of these hormones, peptides, and neurotransmitters and related chemicals associated with very long and extended periods stress —from months to a year or even decades—that could eventually drive us to ill health.

Chronic stress—caused by unhappy marriages, deaths of loved ones, dysfunctional families, hated jobs in which we feel trapped, traumatic childhood situations, war, natural disasters, divorce, and so on—is the problem. Any stressor that continues for more than 3 months is considered long-term and chronic.

For AgnesMary, going to the doctor triggered her stress mechanism, driving her blood pressure sky high. She didn't remain with me long enough to get to the crux of the memories that underpinned her anxiety. After tapping thousands of cases, my educated guess is that the formal atmosphere of her doctor's medical office triggered AgnesMary, along with her physician's level of authority. These were her triggers; much like the green office walls were a trigger for my client mentioned in Chapter 2. AgnesMary was still "rebelling" in her adulthood against her strict dad, and it caused her anxiety on some deep level. Of course, it could also have been a myriad of other subconscious reasons that we never discussed or tapped on, thoughts the Holy Spirit would have eventually revealed had we tapped long enough.

The worst part of chronic stress is we become accustomed to it; we no longer notice it, except for a bit of jitteriness or that occasional explosive habit that makes

27 Church, *The Genie in Your Genes*, 210–211.

us lash out at everyone around us for no apparent reason. We think it's just the way life is. We can do nothing about it. Our habits are just who we are! We are comfortable in our pain.

But do we have to live with these bad habits and problems?

Research now concludes chronic stress can kill us. It can cause heart attacks, strokes, cancer, auto-immune diseases and, diseases that injure other body parts and organs—any of the areas where your body-mind stores emotional damage.[28]

> Dr. Gabor Mate states, "In 1998, *The American Journal of Preventative Medicine* published the results of the Adverse Childhood Experiences (ACE) study. There were over ninety-five hundred adult participants in this research project. Childhood stressors such as emotional or sexual abuse, violence, drug use or mental illness in the family were correlated with adult risk behaviours, health outcomes and death. There was a 'strong graded relationship' between dysfunction in the family of origin and adult health status – that is, the greater the exposure to dysfunction had been in childhood, the worse the health status were in the adult and the greater were the chances of untimely death from cancer, heart disease, injury, and other causes."[29]

AgnesMary's doctor warned that her elevated blood pressure could cause problems if she didn't agree to medication, but she detested more meds. So she had to figure out another way to lower her pressure. Sadly, many times, doctors simply recommend medications not realizing underlying emotional issues are causing the problem. For example, hypertension can be a symptom of a grave emotional disease.

How does all this damage occur without us knowing it's happening? That answer lies deep within God's created physiology, which we look at in the next chapter. But not to worry, we now know the simple solution to some of these emotional and physical issues lies in Christian EFT.

---

28   Ibid., 255–256; Mate, *When the Body Says NO*, 162–163.
29   Mate, *When the Body Says NO*, 276.

CHAPTER 4

Physiology of Stress

Small organs like the hypothalamus, thalamus, pituitary, adrenal glands, amygdala, hippocampus, and other even smaller organs, many of which lie deep within the brain, are responsible for controlling our stress. It is all done automatically— just the way God designed it to work.

Research now shows we have 50 trillion cells in our bodies.[30] Each cell has 10,000 to 100,000 or more cell receptors.[31] A cell receptor is literally a portal or opening from the outside of the cell into its internal core, where metabolism occurs. It is through these cellular receptors that each cell picks up all the nutrients, fluids, and other necessary chemicals it needs to sustain itself.[32]

Interesting to note is each receptor, for the most part, is monogamous. It can only take in one type of chemical, peptide, vitamin, neurotransmitter, and so on. For example, a vitamin B2 receptor cannot accept an estrogen molecule; only a vitamin B2 molecule can get to that receptor.[33]

We now know negative emotions caused by harmful circumstances in our lives clog up these receptors.[34] It appears nothing can get in or out of the receptors once they are damaged. When our body replaces itself totally, cell by cell, about every 7 years, it doesn't give us new cellular receptors. It replaces like with like only. If you have a damaged liver cell, the body replaces that liver cell with another *new* damaged cell, complete with its damaged receptors. If you have enough dam-

---

30 http://scienceblogs.com/gregladen/2011/11/28/how-many-cells-are-there-in-th/
31 Mate, *When the Body Says NO*, 89.
32 www.verywell.com/what-is-a-receptor-on-a-cell-562554
33 Dispenza, *Evolve Your Brain*, 288–289.
34 Pert, *Everything You Need to Know to Feel Go(o)d*, 232.

aged liver cellular receptors, then the liver itself gets sick. It is not easy for it to obtain sufficient nutrition and chemicals to keep it healthy. Multiply those effects by the approximately 60 different organs we have in our body, and the potential for an eventual bodily system failure is quite high.

CELLULAR ANTENNAS

Dr. Joe Dispenza explains this damage: we wear out cell receptors when they are flooded day in and day out with excess stress chemicals, desensitizing us to our emotions, causing us to need more of a chemical rush to keep us going throughout the day.[35]

Dr. Bruce Lipton explains these cell receptors, calling them antennas: God created these "antennas" on the outside of the cell[36] to pay close attention to what is going on inside and outside of all the body's 50,000, 000 cells, closely watching all the signals of both pleasure and danger.[37]

Millions of these antennae exist within our bodies. According to Joe Dispenza, "Every cell has thousands of receptors, and nerve cells have millions of them to serve as sensors."[38] The antennas are like radar, picking up every scrap of sensory information around us, both internal and external. It is speculated that when these projectile organelles get damaged due to an overabundance of negative emotions, they cease to work, causing all manner of chronic diseases. The cells' information center has gone off-line. As the saying goes, no one is minding the store.

Dr. Michael Ruff states: "Memory, as we know, is stored or encoded in cells at the level of the receptor throughout the bodymind. When we experience a traumatic event, physical or psychological, an emotional component of that trauma exists in the body as well as the brain."[39] He continues, "Candace has talked about the notion that the physical self is your subconscious mind. What she's saying is that at the level of the body, you are unaware of your mind. If you're not aware of memories and traumas stored in your bodymind, you can't do anything about them. So the first step in healing or recovery must involve awareness of where your past and injuries are stored, and then making an attempt to unravel them."[40]

35   Dispenza, *Evolve Your Brain*, 310.
36   Ibid., 289.
37   Lipton, *The Biology of Belief*, 53.
38   Dispenza, *Evolve Your Brain*, 288.
39   Pert, *Everything You Need to Know to Feel Go(o)d*, 171.
40   Ibid., 172.

This is exactly what we do when we tap. We search for negative memories and trauma that have been running our life for decades. Dr. Lipton states the same idea: "There is no similar self-awareness operating in the subconscious mind."[41] He continues, "Similarly, we must realize that no amount of yelling or cajoling by the conscious mind can ever change the behavioral 'tapes' programmed into the subconscious mind." He concludes by stating that "willpower is admirable," but success will most likely be limited because the subconscious mind will adhere to the pre-programmed thoughts.[42] We operate the way we were taught to live by those who taught us our ideas.

Besides these antennas or receptors, the brain houses structures like the amygdala, the alarm center of the body, which assists with processing emotions like fear, anger, anxiety, and pleasure.

The amygdala helps the hippocampus, the mind's historian, to decide what memories to store and which memories to let go. The higher the adrenaline level during the event, the more likely the hippocampus will encode and *remember* the event in our cells. If the emotional turmoil is terrifyingly high, the hippocampus simply goes off-line, allowing us to completely "forget" the horrible memory ever happened.

The amygdala controls the fear conditioning feedback loop that often gets us into trouble. It is a Pavlovian response (i.e., dogs salivating when a bell rang indicating food). If a particular noise in our childhood repetitively signaled that our drunken father was home, and we often had a nasty confrontation with him, then that noise or any very similar noise will signal the amygdala that there is danger abreast. This reaction can continue for the remainder of our lives.

All of this is processed subconsciously, and when that signal is received today, you will have the *exact* same physiological response now that you had when you heard your dad walk through the front door decades ago. As we mentioned, this memory process is called triggering. This is what happened to our green pick-up truck client: the accident happened when he was aged 5, but the trigger was still present, trying to protect him from all things of that exact green color!

Our subconscious is extremely literal, linear and logical. It has no sense of humor, nor does it see in shades of gray differentiation. That truck's green color is that green color. The subconscious does not take into consideration the difference be-

41 Lipton, *The Biology of Belief*, 2008, 140.
42 Ibid., 141.

tween an out-of-control vehicle and a quiet, unassuming office wall! It's all green, you know!

An example is today you hear a slamming door—perhaps the wind blew it shut—but your mind doesn't know that fact. So suddenly and without any thought on your part, your heart races, your palms become sweaty, and you tense up waiting for your drunken dad to appear.

Eventually, when you realize it's not your father, your physiological reactions settle down. But if the noise, or trigger, happened frequently as a child, then your body is in a constant state of alert today as an adult. That is chronic stress, subconsciously seated. It's as dangerous and deadly today as it was years ago—when your father came home drunk and fought with you.

AgnesMary's trigger was simply remembering she had a doctor's appointment. Just the thought alone was enough to raise her blood pressure far beyond an acceptable range, according to her doctor. On occasion, AgnesMary would visit a local drugstore to check her own blood pressure. It was nearly always in the normal range—if she had no appointments coming up soon. AgnesMary's biggest issue was her age. She was in her 70's, so she always had another doctor's appointment looming—dentist, podiatrist, or the internist and his endless list of tests and x-rays, which also raised AgnesMary's blood pressure! One compounded the next.

THE LIMBIC SYSTEM

Our limbic system, or our emotional brain, consists of the hypothalamus, thalamus, pituitary, adrenal glands, amygdala, hippocampus, and other small structures. AgnesMary's limbic system would fully engage once she remembered an upcoming doctor's appointment, and it had little to do with the doctor's visit. Instead, it was a trigger from her past. As we tap, Holy Spirit does a wonderful job pointing out where the trigger started. These memories give us practitioners great tapping fodder.

During stress or danger, the mechanism known as the HPA Axis—the hypothalamus-pituitary-adrenal axis—rev us up to cope and deal with danger, perceived or real, as we move quickly to get ourselves out of danger. After the stress is resolved, if the duration is short-term, the PNS relaxes us. High levels of stress inhibits healing and keeps our immune system constantly compromised.[43]

---

43 Mate, *When the Body Says NO*, 36.

The hypothalamus—the H in HPA axis—controls much of our subconscious bodily functions, like temperature control, heart rate, perspiration, sleep, hunger, sex drive, and hormones, along with registering incoming emotions. It is a small organ, but it has great responsibilities. The hypothalamus is a bit like the boss because it controls those involuntary functions we never have to think about.[44]

Our hypothalamus sends a signal to our adrenal glands to pump adrenaline (epinephrine) into the bloodstream. Epinephrine is the stimulant that causes physiological reactions during stress. Adrenaline is often given to asthma attack sufferers to open up the lungs to get them breathing again.

During stress, adrenaline triggers a surge of glucose—blood sugar and fats—into the blood stream to give us energy to deal with danger. This is one reason why stress can lead to obesity or diabetes. Our glucose level never returns to normal, and our pancreas continues to secrete insulin to drive down the sugar level, eventually wearing out the pancreas and necessitating a supplement of insulin or oral medication to keep the blood sugar within normal limits.

AgnesMary's doctor feared her body could potentially suffer from these diseases, compounding her whole physiological problem. Diabetes would exacerbate her hypertension, and her hypertension could cause a stroke or heart attack.

The pituitary gland—the P in HPA axis—is called the master gland, and it is controlled by the hypothalamus. The pituitary gland has two different lobes that control the thyroid, growth hormones, prolactin, which stimulates breast milk, sex hormones, and corticotrophin hormones, which stimulate the adrenal glands to take action. Pituitary also secretes oxytocin, an amazing hormone that stimulates labor, bonding between mother and child, and further bonding in adulthood.

The adrenal glands—the A in HPA axis—sit atop your kidneys and have two distinct parts with different functions. The adrenals supply cortisol, adrenaline, and aldosterone. Cortisol is involved with metabolism. This is why many chronically stressed people easily gain weight, particularly belly fat. Their cortisol and blood sugar levels remain high, completely disrupting their metabolism. Adrenaline, or epinephrine, jumpstarts us when we're stressed, but those chemicals also wear out our adrenals, which eventually leave us with absolutely no resources to cope with any further stress, and aldosterone, which controls our fluid levels.

---

44 Lipton, *The Biology of Belief*, 2008, 118.

AgnesMary was beginning to gain weight, upsetting the equilibrium between that and her blood pressure. This emotional upset that has turned physical begins to look cyclic. One problem exacerbates another.

AN INSIDE JOB

In short term stress, as the danger passes, our cortisol and adrenaline levels slowdown, the PNS kicks in with a blast of endorphins to settle us down even more by lowering our heart rate, blood pressure, breathing rate, allowing us to once again digest food and go about with our daily activities.

Our autonomic nervous system is like car pedals. The SNS is the accelerator, and the PNS is the brake. We press the gas pedal to surge forward and pump the brakes to slow down. Our body revs up with stress and then puts on the brakes, dousing us with endorphins, to de-stress us. Gas, brakes, gas, brakes is how we proceed through life.

SNS hits the accelerator, triggering the FFF mechanism, giving us a burst of energy to get through whatever we see or perceive as danger. Remember, our mind doesn't understand the difference between real problems like a fist coming at our nose and perceived problems like worry. It dispenses the same harmful, over-abundance of chemicals either way. The real danger eventually goes away, and we recover from that stress. But the worry and anxiety from perceived danger is insidious and near constant, eating away at our blood vessels, nerves, and stomach lining.[45]

The PNS puts on the brakes within our nervous system after the danger has passed, relaxing all the bodily structures that were revved up during the stressful event. We relax, our heartbeat regulates, our breathing slows, our full stomach digests, and our muscle tension lessens.

Chronic stress continually keeps the gas accelerator pressed firmly to the floor, going full speed ahead. The body never responds to the quieting endorphins. It never gets the message that the danger has passed. This chronic underlying anxiety is especially prevalent when early in life traumatic events have happened to us. All of these processes happen beneath our conscious awareness. We have no control over any of it, and our mind, body, and emotions never get rested or relaxed—unless we consider giving tapping a try.

---

45 Mate, *When the Body Says NO*, 243.

AgnesMary rarely felt rested. She worried constantly about her elevated blood pressure and the repercussions it would have on her health. All the while the real problem was the early childhood pressure she had never resolved in her mind. She had never forgiven her father for his lack of care and attention and his constant drinking. This long-term subconscious stress from the difficult memories of our past is the bigger danger. And the cause of subconscious stress tends to be earlier traumatic events or memories that happen before age 25, after which the brain fully matures into adulthood.[46]

How do we know those painful memories are still bothering us? Physiological breakdown—either scattered, unconnected symptoms that physicians can't explain or diagnose or full-blown disease—tends to let us know emotional distress could be the cause. The subconscious holds your emotional pain well for 10, 20 or even 30 years before it finally gives up and gives out. When the subconscious wears down and can no longer hold negative memories, it can transfer the emotional pain as physical pain to a body part or organ.

Dr. Candace Pert wrote it pretty clearly when she said:

> *"We're constantly resonating with what we already know to be true* [Pert's italics]. Everything that you feel is filtered along a gradient of past experience and memory that's stored in your receptors – there isn't any absolute or external reality! What you experience as reality is your *story* [Pert's italics] of what happened."[47]

PERCEPTION IS EVERYTHING

When teaching Emotional Freedom Techniques I often say, "In tapping, the truth is irrelevant." That seems like an odd thing for a Christian to say when God specifically commanded us in the Seventh Commandment to always tell the truth! Dr. Pert is correct, 100% correct. We perceive what our truth is on an emotional level. None of that story may have an ounce of truth to it, but we still believe what we feel because it is our life and our belief system and/or perceptions creating our reality.

AgnesMary had a litany of old, negative memories. All of them were her interpretation of what her father's words and actions meant to her. Although she thought she let go of them, tapping revealed high SUDS levels. It was apparent her sub-

---

46 Pert, *Everything You Need to Know to Feel Go(o)d*, 46.
47 Ibid., 54.

conscious had transferred her emotional pain to a physical symptom—based on her negative perception of her childhood years. Hypertension hadn't quite ruined her health yet, but AgnesMary had to be willing to do the tapping work. And there was possibly still time for tapping to take effect.

A process called up-regulation occurs when we are chronically stressed where the body makes more cell receptors to "take up" the excess chemicals we make when we experience the same emotional pain again and again, and it becomes an addictive pattern of life[48], causing us to be *stuck* in life unable to move ahead into what God wants for us. AgnesMary was stuck.

God expects us to take responsibility for ourselves. Genesis 1:28 reads, "God blessed them and said to them, 'Be fruitful and increase in number; fill the earth and subdue it. Rule over the fish in the sea and the birds in the sky and over every living creature that moves on the ground.'" God also meant for us to take dominion over ourselves; therefore, Christians should learn to tap! AgnesMary simply wasn't ready to finish her tapping work. Something in her mind was still holding her back. Sometimes, that self-sabotage kicks in, keeping us locked in our emotional and physical pain.

We must strive to recognize emotional problems before anxiety or worry pervade our lives and before our minds transfer the emotional pain into physical health issues. Tapping can often stop the emotional pain from progressing. God has also given us tapping to release psychological trauma and its effects *permanently*; however, we must be willing to do the tapping work.

LIQUID QUARTZ CRYSTALS

Humans have liquid quartz crystals[49] in every cell of our bodies[50]; therefore, as we tap we create a low voltage (piezoelectric) charge throughout the lowest layer of our skin (fascia) and connective tissue—found in between other tissues everywhere in the body including the central nervous system that includes the brain and spinal cord—because these crystals respond to pressure and stimulation.[51] Some scientists even believe the body's acupuncture points act like amplifiers,

---

48 Dispenza, *Evolve Your Brain*, 302.
49 Kelly, *The Human Antenna*, 65; Church, *The Genie in Your Genes*, 146–148.
50 www.i-sis.org.uk/lcm.php
51 Pert, *Everything You Need to Know to Feel Go(o)d*, 195.

pushing this tunable vibration along the meridians, which touch nearly every cell of our human body.[52]

In theory, these vibrations do several things, such as inform our amygdala and hippocampus that we are now safe because the danger is past; the signal soothes those organs.[53] Secondly, it is surmised, it cleans out cellular receptors that have become blocked due to years of carrying negative emotions, possibly reviving those cells back to their original functioning capacity. This is the research of Dr. Candace Pert, among others.

Because the liquefied quartz reaches most, if not all, areas of our body, it sends a healing, quieting message spoken from an electromagnetic place that relaxes us. This moves us into slower alpha and theta brainwave states, whereby our cortisol levels drop, allowing our DHEA (dehydroepiandrosterone—a hormone made by the adrenal glands) level to rise.

We must have adequate levels of DHEA to restore and heal our bodies, keeping our immune system in tip-top shape. If the DHEA level is high (where we want it to be), cortisol has to be low. Conversely, if the cortisol level is high, then the DHEA level is low.[54]

A low DHEA level will eventually cause us to become ill. It is low because we are under stress, and pumping out too much cortisol, drowning out the DHEA. In reality, the same precursor molecule that makes cortisol also makes DHEA, so when the body has to make an overabundance of cortisol, there are not enough precursor molecules left to make DHEA.

So how can we maintain an optimal level of healing? That answer seems pretty simple. We give tapping a try!

I often wish AgnesMary would have used EFT on her own between appointments, and that she would have allowed me to finish tapping with her, as I know from working with so many others how beneficial Emotional Freedom Techniques is for both our physical and emotional health.

---

52 For information about meridians, please visit http://upliftconnect.com/science-proves-meridians-exist/
53 Church, *The Genie in Your Genes*, 231.
54 Ibid., 75.

Tapping accomplishes many healing benefits because that is the way God created EFT to work. He knew we would need some help! Tapping relaxes us, raising our DHEA level, while telling our amygdala and hippocampus that the harmful, harsh events of the past are over and done with, and informing our mind we are safe today.

We know how much of the neurochemistry works, but exactly how EFT resolves these problems physiologically remains theoretic. Personally, I subscribe to the idea that if something is hot, bright orange, glowing, and it looks like a fire, it most probably is fire. So, if Dr. Candace Pert says negative emotions block our cell receptor, with disease to follow, and tapping on certain acupuncture points amplifies a quartz vibration throughout the body, allowing us to heal, then I am going to conclude for myself that tapping must unblock plugged cell receptors to once again allow our bodies to absorb all the nutrients it needs to get and stay healthy.

We do know that stimulating the correct acupuncture points while under stress does result in a lower heart rate, and lowered anxiety and pain.[55]

We speculate how God heals; we simply don't totally understand the mechanisms. However, we do know healing occurs, as anecdotal evidence appears to show, and we know God created it to happen when we use tapping for physical and emotional problems. In the end, does it really matter how God heals us? He is God, and I suspect it will take an eternity to begin to understand all of His thoughts, ideas, and processes.

EFT neutralizes the emotional charge of old traumatic memories that causes us stress, anxiety, and worry today. It is in that stress neutralization that our bodies seem to heal, releasing the anxiety and worry about both the past and the future. It is in this place that we are able to experience what God planned for us since the beginning of time—lives full of inexpressible joy and peace that surpasses all understanding (1 Peter 1:8; Philippians 4:7). This was His original intention![56]

---

55 Ibid., 126–127.
56 To learn more about how God created the stress process to work, check out these videos:
    www.youtube.com/watch?v=v-t1Z5-oPtU&nohtml5=False
    www.youtube.com/watch?v=sQj6GMrt8EE&nohtml5=False

SECTION TWO:
EFT for CHRISTIANS

SUB-SECTION ONE:
EFT for Christians Explained

CHAPTER 5

What is Christian EFT?

Life is life. Stuff happens. We cannot avoid international news, politics, auto accidents, financial setbacks, divorce, family deaths, unemployment, and the endless list goes on. You know what I'm talking about. And then we have those friends who seem to thrive on spouting unceasing stories of mishaps and mayhem. Some people thrive on this negativity. Where's the positive news? There never seems to be enough of it to go around! Well, let me give you a bit of ***good news*** now.

Emotional Freedom Techniques for Christians is the upbeat news when it comes to the issue of stress, anxiety and all other types of negative emotions in our lives. We cannot change what is going on around us or what's happened in the past, but we can work on what goes on *inside* us today! God has ordained a way within our created bodies for us to allow our negative emotions to drain away, hopefully saving us from a litany of future ailments. And this self-help tool is based on biblical truth, Jesus' promises to us, and our affirmations of love and unwavering trust in God—everything we need to heal old wounds while becoming closer to the Lord.

Remember: it is our God who created the intricacies of our physical functions. He engineered the mechanisms, but we are the ones who activate them within our own bodies. We have a choice. He gave us Jesus to redeem us spiritually, so we must accept Jesus' control in our lives to redeem us physically and emotionally, too. He has given us a way to repair the damage we cause ourselves, and the emotional damage others impose *on* us. But we must step out in faith and engage Christian EFT, and use it regularly.

For the uninitiated, I will give the briefest of EFT explanations, including a few visuals to quickly help you understand how to tap. *If you are unfamiliar with the approach in its totality, please refer to my first book, EFT for Christians.*[57]

Emotional Freedom Techniques is a part of the field of energy medicine and energy psychology, which is based on the foundation that good health relies on the proper energy flow throughout the body. Any major stressor can interrupt this flow, creating an energy "block" that can lead to disease.[58] Here we will just highlight a few of the more important parts of tapping: SUDS scale, tapping points, and the set-up statements.

We have several approaches from which to choose to learn how to tap on unwanted habits and behaviors; there is usually a way to get to most unwanted emotions using EFT. This is one of the reasons I suggest to everyone truly interested in knowing how to use EFT to take a tapping class or classes[59] with a certified EFT Practitioner/Trainer. There are so many nuances of how to get to the root and bottom of what is really going on in a client's life, or even in the life of an individual who wants to use EFT as a tool to move closer to God, changing behaviors to be more like Jesus.

As you will find in most EFT instructions, we use a scale called the SUD scale, or Subjective Units of Distress Scale, to measure the intensity of our emotions or physical pain. Below is an illustration of how the SUD Scale works.

---

57 Basic tapping instructions are also available for free downloading from www. GloryWaves.org/EFT.

58 https://thetruthaboutcancer.com/emotional-freedom-technique-cancer/?gl=58282 7118&mpweb=144-1397290-160752257.

59 www.eftforchristians.com/classes.html

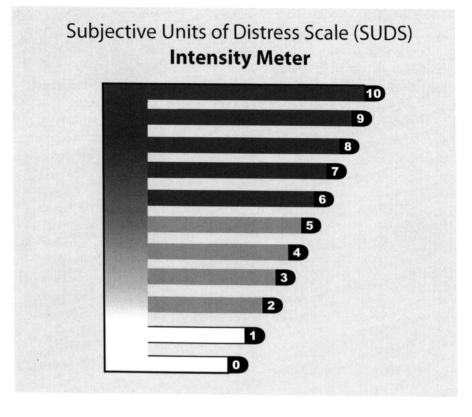

DEFINING THE INTENSITY OF THE PROBLEM

EFT sessions usually begin with a self-estimate of intensity, or discomfort of an emotion or pain we are feeling, using a scale from zero to 10. This is the SUD scale. The discomfort measured can be physical like headache pain or a craving, or it can be an emotion like fear, anxiety, depression, or anger.

It's always best to assign a scale number to each emotion and physical pain that comes up before and after you tap, so you can readily determine how much progress you're making. Since tapping evokes past events and memories, it's important to assess your intensity as it exists *now* rather than when the event or problem first occurred.

Don't worry if you find it difficult to select an exact number at first—whether a 5 or a 6, or a 2 or a 3. Using the 0-to-10 intensity meter becomes easier and more automatic with practice. To get started, simply assign yourself a number. It helps to remind yourself there are no wrong answers in tapping. Guessing an intensity number will work fine for novices. The number is simply a benchmark for comparison during and after the tapping session.

For reference, jot down the number and add a few notes. For example, if you're focusing on a particular physical pain, write down where the pain is located, how it interferes with your range of motion, and whether it hurts more when you move to the left or right, stand or sit, and so forth.

Note: with children, it may be best to indicate intensity by stretching one's arms wide apart for major pain and bringing them close together for minor pain. Children find it easier to express "big" and "small" with their hands than with a number scale. The method you choose doesn't matter as long as it works for you.

THE ACUPRESSURE TAPPING POINTS

(See details on next page.)

USING THE CHRISTIAN SETUP

When tapping with Christians new to EFT, I like to explain to them the two-part "setup phrase," as mentioned in the introduction of this book. In the first part we acknowledge the negative emotion we're feeling. In the second part of this setup statement, we affirm we love ourselves in spite of ourselves. For example, "I deeply and completely accept myself." Many times I find they're uncomfortable with this second part because, often, they have been hurt deeply and are unable to affirm any love to themselves. Therefore, the affirmation can easily be modified to something like: "I will possibly sometime in the future consider accepting myself." All we are doing is stating that perhaps we can accept things just as they are, or that maybe it's a possibility for the future. There is no correct or incorrect way to state this acceptance.

Gary Craig, founder of EFT, originally used the setup statement to counter possible "psychological reversal." Psychological reversal is often manifested in two ways. First, some people carry around self-sabotaging tendencies. For example, they may begin many projects, but they never seem able to finish any of them. Why? Something lodged in their subconscious mind stops them because it is somehow dangerous to finish whatever they started. This phenomenon is a form of procrastination.

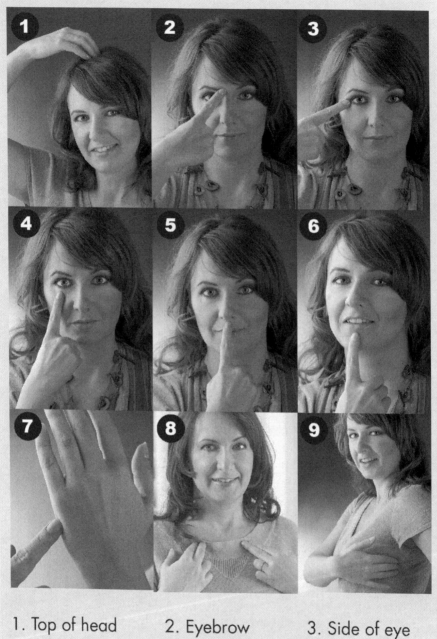

1. Top of head
2. Eyebrow
3. Side of eye
4. Under eye
5. Under nose
6. Chin
7. Karate chop
8. Collarbone
9. Under arm

Secondly, many people feel little or no emotional response to something extremely negative that happened in their lives. They completely shut down their feelings or are entirely dissociated from them. Psychological reversal will slow down EFT's healing process, or it can stop it completely. Therefore, we use the setup statement to counteract the effects of this obstacle.

During EFT, the setup statement helps clarify and identify precisely what is the problem, event, or emotion being tapped on. It is standard in the basic EFT protocol, and it has been well-researched over the years. It just works, so we have no need to mess with a proven process!

An example of the standard two-part setup phrase is this: "Even though I have this problem, I deeply and completely accept myself."

The first part states the problem, and the second part is the affirmation or acceptance. In *EFT for Christians,* I personally recommend using a Christian acceptance statement of your own choice that specifically resonates with you. It is important to note, however, that it is the actual physical tapping that clears out the problem you are addressing.

Following are a few setup phrase examples. You can use or modify them, or feel free to create your own. There are no right or wrong statements, per se. Just be sure to include the two parts: The exposure or problem statement ("Even though") and the affirmation or acceptance statement (e.g., "God loves me and will heal me").

> *Even though I remember when my sister pushed me off the bed, splitting my lip on that wooden dresser, and I felt really hurt by that both physically and emotionally, I know Jesus loves me and therefore I accept myself with all these feelings, just the way I am.*
>
> *Even though I feel all this anger in my heart for all the pain my husband has caused me all these years, I would like to let all of this go because I know God loves me very much and He expects me to eventually forgive Dave, and maybe someday I can do that.*
>
> *Even though I feel all this tightness in my throat, and I wish I could simply state what I really feel about that awful accident 12 years ago, I hope someday God will help me to let all this resentment go, and give me a peace about all that has happened around that trauma.*

> *Even though my entire life seems like an emotional mess and I blame my parents for absolutely all of it, I would like to believe God can fix all of this, and that He could someday allow my hurt to heal, and to open up a river of forgiveness in this poor heart of mine toward my parents.*

Stating the setup phrase in your own words with your own personalized problem alerts your subconscious to exactly what you want dealt with as you tap. It often clarifies and aids in focusing on those exact details your body feels around this particular problem. It's the specificity that intensifies and points EFT to the problem for you.

From the setup sentence, you extrapolate your "reminder" phrases, which are all the things you say as you tap each acupressure point.

The reminder statement that is used for the actual tapping of the acupuncture or acupressure points can be either as simple as stating the emotion you feel such as, *"This anger," "This resentment,"* or *"This hurt,"* or it can focus instead on the physical feelings you're experiencing, such as, *"This tightness in my chest," "This squeezing sensation in my heart,"* or *"This nausea in my stomach."* You may also use a piece of the memory such as, *"My sister pushed me," "My parents were so mean,"* or *"That car accident."*

You may choose to add in your own personal Christian belief touches to the reminder statement, such as, *"I cover this anger with the blood of my Savior Jesus," "I let this resentment go in the name of Jesus,"* or *"I give all this pain to my Lord Jesus as He already bore it on the cross for me."*

While there are no correct or incorrect words, it's important to understand that using general scripts from the Internet won't yield the same results as your own personalized tapping. Those scripts aren't specific to *your* emotional problem. While you may achieve some limited relief, when you personalize the words to identify your specific feelings, the tapping will resonate deeply, accomplishing positive results much more quickly and effectively.[60]

---

60   We invite you to download Scripture Protocols and Visionary Inner Healing Techniques for Tapping FREE from www.GloryWaves.org/EFT.

CHAPTER 6

Why Should Christians Use EFT?

This book is written to positively challenge you, the born-again Christian, to consider learning a skill that can possibly revolutionize your life and the lives of all those around you. Boldly, in my experience, Emotional Freedom Techniques has worked well for me. While I cannot provide any guarantees, I have many case studies of lives apparently changed by tapping based on testimonials I have received. This is God's way of healing. He "invented" it! He put this healing process into our very physiology. He wants us, His children, to heal and to serve Him all the days of our lives.

I'm often asked, "Why should I use EFT when I have God Who can heal me?"

God heals supernaturally and naturally. We've all heard stories of a person who was prayed over for a cigarette addiction and never smoked again. That is God working supernaturally. That is what constitutes a true life *miracle*, like the ones Jesus performed during His tenure here on earth.

But sometimes there is a part we get to play in our breakthrough. For example, I struggled with emotional issues for 40 years before I found freedom. God used the gift of EFT to transform my life. He allowed the natural process that He set in motion at the time of Creation to unfold. This is called a *healing*.

There's a difference between these two—a miracle and a healing. Miracles happen instantaneously; healings simply take some time. Healing works itself out in the course of God's natural creation. It takes time to reveal a healing. Healing is a miracle in slower motion!

While God does *not* cause our pain, He can redeem it. God is a good and loving Father and He does NOT put cancer on people to teach them a lesson! However, He can use the pain and circumstances we encounter in this fallen world and teach us through them. Sometimes, emotional pain holds some of these life lessons.

Often God has a bigger plan for our lives (Jeremiah 29:11), something we could never ever imagine. Steven Curtis Chapman's song "Glorious Unfolding" expresses this exact idea—God has a plan for us! A purpose we most likely might not have volunteered for, or dreamed of, but a purpose that fits inside His most perfect will for us.

God uses everyone. In fact, I often believe, He takes the most unsuspecting person to do His mighty work. The pretentious, haughty, know-it-alls of the world tend to be of no use to God. He can't get their attention. He is looking for the committed, silent, humble servants to move His purposes ahead in the Kingdom. These servants sit back, surrender, pray, study God's Word, and ask Him what He requires of them. They wait and watch God work for His greater glory and our greater good!

In this greater good, God often brings healing to us, which opens up a huge awareness of hindsight in our thinking. Like Joseph we can say "You intended to harm me, but God intended it for good to accomplish what is now being done, the saving of many lives" (Genesis 50:20). The Lord redeems our suffering "and we know that in all things God works for the good of those who love Him, who have been called according to His purpose" (Romans 8:28).

> God asks us in James 5:14–16, *"Is anyone among you sick? Let them call the elders of the church to pray over them and anoint them with oil in the name of the Lord. And the prayer offered in faith will make the sick person well; the Lord will raise them up. If they have sinned, they will be forgiven."*

Can God still heal by anointing with oil and the laying on of hands? I believe whole-heartedly He can, but the problem today is unbelief across the globe, especially in western culture. We are so imbued with the amazing effectiveness of western medicine that we assume God has replaced His supernatural healing with the "miracle" of medical care today. I'm certainly not saying to stop using doctors. Doctors are God's healing tools, too! If I had stomach pain, thinking I had appendicitis, I couldn't get to a surgeon's office fast enough, as that appendix must be removed, and tapping is not a surgical tool!

God instructs us in Matthew 17:20 *we must have faith, "Because you have so little faith. Truly I tell you, if you have faith as small as a mustard seed, you can say to this mountain, 'Move from here to there,' and it will move. Nothing will be impossible for you."*

Christians today are made to believe miracles stopped after the early apostolic church. Many of us, therefore, assume God has given us modern medicine to replace miracles. I've even heard preachers go so far as to explain that God used miracles back in the First Century strictly because we didn't have the medical and scientific knowledge we have today. To believe biblical miracles happened only because of medical ignorance, which modern-day "advanced" medicine has surpassed, limits the greatness of God.

We often need both doctors and tapping. Science seems to be showing us that tapping makes for "preventative medicine" and can be "pro-active" for your own health.

God is as magnificent a Caregiver today as He was in the time of the apostles. He has never changed (Hebrews 13:8), our attitudes have.

EFT can be used in addition to modern medicine. I know few of us who would forego a doctor's visit when we are sick. Often physical ailments have a huge emotional basis. Tapping often discovers and eliminates the emotional core of the physical problem.

My disclaimer is this: If you require medical care, please make an appointment with your physician. Tapping is not a substitute for a medical doctor, especially during medical emergencies. It is imperative you take personal care of your own emotional and physical needs, Christian EFT practitioners see clients who have symptomology but whose doctors haven't been able to diagnose a specific ailment or specific underlying issues.

EFT practitioners see clients who report non-specific symptoms, as the body's "cry for help." Their symptoms were like flashing yellow warning lights, telling us danger is up ahead. Physical symptoms point back to screaming emotional symptoms.

Drs. Bruce Lipton, Robert Scaer, Peter Levine, Daniel Siegel, Joe Dispenza, Bessel van der Kolk, Daniel Amen, Candace Pert, and Caroline Leaf all understand and tout the connection among emotions, trauma, and our physical health.

In addition to addressing our physical wellbeing, EFT can offer us several other positive results. Following are the reasons we Christians *should* use tapping. I will list them singly, and then explain them in more detail.

EFT changes our perspective of our eternal God.
EFT is a healing modality from God's arsenal.
EFT eliminates our shame-based life, which was started by Adam and Eve in the Garden.

EFT changes our perspective of God. If all we know is abandonment, fault-finding, ridicule, and abuse, how can we understand the nature of our loving God? Our God sent Jesus, His only Son, to earth to die in a shame-filled way on a lonely wooden cross for our sins. He sacrificed His Son in order that we become reconciled to Him, becoming a child of His, and inheriting His Kingdom of Heaven.

We cannot possibly understand this if our own earthly father beat us to within an inch of our lives routinely for our infractions as children. Additionally, we seem never to learn. We tend to think we can do life alone—life with all of its complications and unseen hazards, succumbing to the belief we are smarter than God.

Once we choose to apply EFT to our life to address our father's abuse against us, God's gift of forgiveness often begins to flow through our hearts. We learn to forgive our father, albeit slowly at times. We then begin to understand the loving and caring nature of our heavenly Father.

God is not a vindictive God. God is not a punishing God. God loves you more than anything in the entire universe. He sacrificed His own son, so you can become one of His children. John 3:16 states, "For God so loved the world that he gave his one and only Son, that whoever believes in him shall not perish but have eternal life." It is a love we may never quite understand, but it is a love we all so desperately need.

And once we switch our prayer life from one of supplication to one of thanksgiving, our perspective of God changes even more. As God blesses us more and more, giving us a peace and joy filled life (Romans 5:1; John 16:33), we understand in our hearts what an amazing God we serve. As EFT changes our perception about the bad things in life, tapping changes our perception of Who God is and how much He loves us. EFT for Christians makes this a package deal. Your internal spiritual life will change and improve with tapping. The less negative junk you have in your life, the more room you have for God's joy and peace. Both cannot co-exist in you because you simply don't have enough space in your heart for it all. Lose all of life's junk and watch as you gain God's goodness and peace.

EFT is a healing modality from God's arsenal. As with just about everything we touch, we grabbed tapping from God's arsenal and turned it into a human healing procedure, often removing any semblance of God's involvement in it. We sometimes don't stop to give God the credit due for His healing because we have a "we can do it ourselves" mentality inherited from Adam and Eve. We love to do this. We love to play God. Adam and Eve tried it in the Garden of Eden, and it didn't work out well for them at all.

In my experience, tapping works best within the heart of a Jesus-following Christian. The healing process is quicker because we allow Holy Spirit to do much of the heavy lifting, so we Christians get the best of both worlds! We often get the human bodily healing, but we also get an advanced dose of God's spiritual healing tossed into the tapping mix. It goes hand in hand.

God created us as a unit—our body and spirit were made to function together (Romans 12:4–5). Our bodies are symbolic of how God created the Church. Each part makes up the whole. We function as one. Each piece has its own special job to do. If one body part is healthy, other parts also tend to be healthy. Spiritually, it's no different. God forgives our sins, and He often blesses us physically with good health (3 John 2).

Often we don't consider what a Christian worldview encompasses. For those of us raised in the Church, no matter our Christian denomination, we get Jesus. We understand on some level His message to love one another and do no harm. We understand He is omnipotent, omniscient, omnipresent—a God Who loves us and is able to do anything and everything.

We understand surrender gives us an amazing freedom! God runs our life. All we must do is pay attention and be mindful—the very thing EFT excels at teaching us to do! People who want to run their own show and do their own thing, believe doing so is freedom. No rules, no laws = freedom. But that is so far from the truth, and Christians know better.

Healing is God's purview. Jesus' ministry showcased how healing was done. He told His apostles to go out and heal in His name. Matthew 10:1 states, "Jesus called his twelve disciples to him and gave them authority to drive out impure spirits and to heal every disease and sickness." That imperative still stands for us today.

In fact, Jesus told us we would do greater things than He did! John 14:12–14 reads, "Very truly I tell you, whoever believes in me will do the works I have been doing, and they will do even greater things than these, because I am going to the Father. And I will do whatever you ask in my name, so that the Father may be glorified in the Son. You may ask me for anything in my name, and I will do it." Through EFT, God is just getting started.

He is calling us to work the greater things promised. The world is in desperate need of healing, and who better to heal than the Church! We can take EFT to higher heights than any of us ever expected it to go because Jesus said that is our job. In order for us Christians to do that, we must have our own personal emotional houses in order, eliminating shame and other negative emotions. Tapping will accomplish that very thing via His process of sanctification.

HELEN'S STORY – A TOXIC COMBINATION OF PERFECTIONISM AND SHAME

Dee Whitaker LeGrand[61] is a Believer who is a dedicated EFT practitioner and coach. She has worked with hundreds of Christian men, women, and children over the past several years in the area of restorative Christian EFT. She has witnessed firsthand the healing of worry, stress, and anxiety and the underlying issues of inner emotional wounds, triggers, and physical ailments. Here is one of Dee's case studies.

There was a lot of anxiety about the constant shameful thoughts that plagued Helen growing up in a family that strived for success. Her father had been raised during the Depression and was determined to be prosperous financially. He proved himself as an entrepreneur from an early age, opening multiple businesses in different economic sectors and pouring all his energy, attention, and time into making them profitable. Every little thing always had to be perfect.

He carried this attitude into his family's environment, too. So Helen and her sisters were always being reprimanded for anything that was less than perfect. When they went out, their father would show them off to his business colleagues and their wives, displaying them as perfect children with perfect manners. Helen felt she lived in a goldfish bowl, always being watched and constantly reprimanded for even the slightest failing. She quickly learned to never anger her father or disappoint her mother, who also took her perfectionistic cues from him to avoid suffering the wrath of her "perfect" husband.

When I first started working with Helen, I noticed that if she said or did something that, in her mind, was in even the smallest way different from others, she would feel like a bad girl. I decided to tap with Helen on this particular belief just to see what was underneath. This produced a long page of notes recapping different memories that arose from her childhood as she remembered feeling certain she had been a very bad little girl. We took them on one by one in our tapping sessions. Toward the end of each session, I would guide her to ask Jesus to come to her and heal her.

When we first worked on bringing Jesus into our tapping sessions, the words that the Holy Spirit prompted me to say came so fast she could barely follow:

"Even though I'm struggling to feel like Jesus took all my sins to the cross, I have been forgiven, and I am open to the possibility that I can forgive myself."

"Even though I feel shame and unforgiveness toward myself and my parents, and I feel it in my throat, because I was never allowed to talk about this, I am open to accepting myself, and loving myself, just as Jesus accepts me and loves me."

"Even though part of me is holding on to feeling unloved, the rest of me is open to the possibility that God loves me with an unfailing love. 'You, Lord, are forgiving and good, abounding in love to all who call to you.'" (Psalm 86:5)

"My conscience is clear, but that does not make me innocent. It is the Lord who judges me." (1 Corinthians 4:4)

And as she began to release her negative emotions, we tapped on Galatians 5:22 about releasing Christ's healing emotions of love, joy, and peace within her.

We tapped in praise: *"For you created my inmost being; you knit me together in my mother's womb. I praise you because I am fearfully and wonderfully made; your works are wonderful, I know that full well"* (Psalm 139:13–14).

As the intensity of her emotions subsided, we tapped about Jesus going to the cross for her sins—even though she did not feel Jesus did this *for her*. Because of her emotionally absent parents, she didn't receive the love and compassion she needed; therefore, she couldn't imagine Jesus loving her specifically. This time, I asked her to pray during our session and she prayed for the love and forgiveness of Jesus over and over, as though she did not deserve anything from her Savior.

In our next session, she was telling me about her week at work, and how badly it had gone because of her bad behavior. I had sensed for some time that there was a deep shameful event that was holding her back, so I asked if she thought she was ready to acknowledge and release it. Shame is one of the most toxic emotions we carry.

In Helen's case, her mother was uncomfortable in the lifestyle of wealth her husband had created for her and felt she didn't belong in this privileged world. She passed those feelings and emotions on to Helen. Nothing was ever good enough. She was constantly criticizing Helen if she didn't behave perfectly.

Perfection and shame are a toxic combination. This leads right into the territory of thinking you are never good enough, always feeling like a failure, and that, as a Christian, you could never forgive yourself for any feelings or actions you believe are wrong.

Helen talked about the unforgiveness and shame she felt had been foisted on her by her parents, as well as her inability to forgive herself for feeling and acting this way. These thoughts and emotions had turned her into a very critical woman, and rarely a day went by when she was not ashamed of her outbursts at work, or by her caustic remarks to a colleague or employee. It was evident her emotional triggers were very deep. Even though we tapped on them, we were not making a lot of progress. By the Holy Spirit's prompting, I knew there was a stronghold of shame, which had not yet surfaced.

As I guided her to tap about memories of shame she could recall, her tone markedly changed to that of a little girl. She told me she remembered when she was seven and spent time at a summer camp with her 8-year-old friend, Lizzie. They took a shower together that evening and Lizzie showed Helen how to rub up against her. Helen felt something strange and exciting. At her age, she had no idea what it was, but later she wanted to feel that same sensation again. She found this made her feel better after her mom had yelled at her earlier in the day. She continued with this pattern whenever there was turmoil in the household.

Later, she started touching herself at school, still not knowing what it was, but knowing that it took away the feeling of being emotionally detached from her parents; the feeling of not ever being good enough. Even when the teacher saw her touching herself in class and quietly told her to stop, she could not, which resulted in her feeling even more shame.

This continued on until the 6th grade when she met a new friend, Amanda. She shared her secret with Amanda, and Amanda started crying, telling Helen she too had the same shameful problem and wanted to stop. Amanda was Catholic and told Helen they must pray to Mother Mary, and she prayed for both of them while holding Helen's hand. As they prayed, Helen was also asking Mother Mary to please, please allow her to be a good girl again.

After the prayer and healing and confessing sins to each other, Helen stopped and did not have the urge to touch herself again for a long while. When she was 15, she came home distraught after having a fight with a girl at school. She tried to tell her mom about it, but her mom shut her down. So she went to her room and then remembered something that would make her feel better, and by then understood what she was doing, but continued touching and rubbing herself until she felt that old familiar release.

Immediately afterward, she became hysterical and criticized herself over and over; she should have never done that; Jesus did not love her when she did that, and once again, in her mind, she proved to herself and to Jesus she was a bad girl. She also believed she had ruined the rest of her life with her selfish act. And, of course, Helen had never told anyone else about this secret until this tapping session unearthed it.

We then tapped on every part of that memory to release it. When she got down to a SUDS of 1 on all aspects, I asked her to tap and pray to Jesus and ask for His forgiveness, and see if she could totally accept it. She prayed, talking to Him, but not begging Him as she had before, but now speaking as someone who trusted Him, and loved Him. Tears were streaming down my face as a privileged witness to what was happening in Helen's heart after she'd suffered all those decades of pain and self-recrimination.

She finally let go of her shame and let God into her heart fully. That day began her journey of walking in light and love. She told me in a recent session that they'd notice something different about her at the children's center where she volunteers—a lightness and a love for herself and others. Helen is slowly taking in the fact that she's healing, now seeing her younger self as a good girl and herself as a good woman who has a big heart, and a lot of love to give.

As I take my clients through the Christian EFT tapping process, I believe forgiveness is the most important step toward healing and letting go of worry and anxiety. When we are worrying about what's ahead, we are not present—and we are not in the presence of God. As a client once said to me, "You helped me learn the steps to forgiveness so that I can now allow God to clean the window to my heart and soul…so that I can see in.

Shame was one of the first emotions felt by Adam and Eve after disobeying God in the Garden of Eden. In Genesis Chapter 3, they realized after eating the fruit from the Tree of Good and Evil that they were naked, and "they were ashamed."

Adam and Even hid from God. When God questioned this, Adam explained, "I was afraid because I was naked" (Genesis 3:10). Shame and fear all within one Biblical verse. Fear is that base emotion that underlies most all of human behavior. And fear is one of those many emotions tapping can eliminate so very well.

Because of that sin of disobedience in the Garden, we all inherit that shame-based original sin from our first parents. Our sin nature is a loss of the intimacy Adam and Eve had with God. It can be restored to us when we accept Jesus as our Savior. The relationship with God is repaired. The rift is healed.

However, we still carry around in some manner that shame Adam and Eve experienced when they disobeyed God. Shame comes down through family lines when the generation before us has not dealt with the sins and mistakes in their own family (see more in Chapter 16).

EFT can be a process to help eliminate much of the familial shame-based behaviors that haunt many of us from time immemorial.

CHAPTER 7

Holy Spirit Journey

The Holy Spirit is alive! As church-attending Christians, we are taught to believe this. But what does the Holy Spirit actually do?

I was raised in the Roman Catholic Church, so we prayed to the "Holy Ghost." You can imagine the images that drummed up for me as a child! As my school years passed, I never truly grasped much of an understanding of Who the Third person of the Trinity was. I knew the various references in Bible stories. I understood Pentecost. I understood the Virgin Birth, and never questioned it. But now I understand how I developed these early beliefs and how they were put into place for me.

"Give me a child until age seven, and we will have him for life." While there are variations on this quote, it is most often attributed to St. Ignatius and the Jesuits. In Catholicism, at the age of seven we were considered to have reached the "age of reason," whatever that meant to me fifty-five years ago. So at seven years of age, we were permitted our first confession to the local parish priest and allowed to receive First Holy Communion. Adults considered us old enough to understand right from wrong, and the black-robed Benedictine nuns taught us this in "religion" class every school day. The St. Joseph Baltimore Catechism was drummed into our heads by rote memorization, and like many other children in America in Sunday school, we had to stand before a nun and recite those memory verses.

None of us owned a Bible, or an actual catechism book, just those purple mimeographed sheets of paper that stained the hands of the teacher and all of us children. I assumed God's Word was the word of the priest or the nun who I understood to represent Him. We were nearly scared to even think about opening a Bible to take a peek. It was like the Jewish tabernacle—too sacred to even enter

EFT FOR CHRISTIANS   TAPPING INTO GOD'S PEACE AND JOY

into it! And we were told we had no need to own a Bible, as the nuns and priest would teach us all we had to know.

So, what was the Holy Spirit doing all those years to me? Looking back clarity comes. He was standing right beside me, attempting to get my attention all the while protecting me from myself, as He prepared me for the job He had for me 50 years later.

As I look back now, I am astounded at what I see happening to me, emotionally and spiritually, and I suspect He could be doing the same to you, or you would not be reading this book right now!

As an 8-year-old child lying awake in bed at night, I wondered if I was good enough to go to heaven if I died that night. What a question for a little girl to ponder when I should have fallen instantly asleep!

My best guess now is that came from the depths of despair of my early abuse and the death of my baby sister, Karen. God was already stirring my soul. The Holy Spirit was plumbing the depths of what I believed. He was priming the pumps of what would be done with my despair, sadness, and grief.

Fast forward to 8 years ago when my youngest brother, Bill, was struck with leukemia at the age of 46. That event catapulted me back to my younger years of pondering the larger questions of God and heaven. When Bill died 2 years later, I was again left devastated, confused, and bereft of any feelings whatsoever. I was completely numb! What in the world, Lord, are You thinking and doing? How can life be this meaningless?

As I look back now, I see how those 50 years were my boot camp, my training for what is happening now. I had to do that to do this!

This new Sherrie has been commissioned, through the Holy Spirit, to bring Emotional Freedom Techniques and tapping to the Christian world, as a tool of healing physically and emotionally, and a tool of restoration to both the Church and to the dying world. We, the Church, have forgotten our mission. Most of us personally live in so much pain, emotional pain in particular, that we have no energy, ambition or will to do anything but survive day to day within our own lives.

This is what I learned in the St. Joseph Baltimore Catechism nearly 6 decades ago. Question 6 of this catechism asks the question, "Why did God make you?" That answer I have never forgotten: "God made me to know Him, to love Him, and to serve Him in this world, and to be happy with Him forever in heaven."

If that answer is what you desire in your life, here and now, I want to give you all the reasons why you need to incorporate Christian EFT into your daily life, improving your walk with Jesus to bring you into the abundance He talked about throughout Scripture (John 10:10). If you want peace, joy, and contentment in the Lord, read on. EFT can be your skill and tool!

CHAPTER 8

Role of Holy Spirit

The Holy Spirit has rarely received much billing—as I experienced for most of my Christian life, including my years of parochial school education. Frankly, I don't think anyone knew exactly what to do with Him. The Holy Spirit was discussed at the time of my confirmation, but even then He still seemed to be this tagalong Person of the Trinity who had little to do.

He was simply ignored as that Third person of the Trinity. We Christians are clear about the roles of the Father and the Son, but the Holy Spirit? Isn't He that little tongue of fire that appears during Pentecost or that cute dove in Trinity depictions?

As a born-again Spirit-filled Christian, I understand the Holy Spirit is integral to how Emotional Freedom Techniques works within us and the physiology as created by God the Father.

Even though unbelievers will never credit our awesome God or the Holy Spirit with any of their healing, He is faithful and He still heals them because He loves the unbeliever as much as He loves us, and "He makes His sun rise on the evil and on the good, and sends rain on the just and on the unjust" (Matthew 5:45).

The major role of the Holy Spirit is to be the one to quicken us to be like Jesus. He is the Revealer who shows us what we must tap on to change and to become more like our Lord. Holy Spirit partners with us in this transformative process of sanctification, which we cover in detail in the chapter that follows.

The Holy Spirit is our "intuition." It is He Who speaks to us through tapping. I open every Christian EFT session with prayer, and I specifically ask the Holy

Spirit to sit right beside the client and me, whispering in our ears what we need to know and understand around the events and memories we tap on.

I want the Holy Spirit's interpretation of what is going on within our very soul and spirit. He understands us to our core. He knows how many hairs we have on our heads, and He knew us before we were conceived (Luke 12:7; Jeremiah 1:5).

Amazing breakthroughs have happened while tapping with clients and I credit it *all* to the Holy Spirit. "May God himself, the God of peace, sanctify you through and through. May your whole spirit, soul and body be kept blameless at the coming of our Lord Jesus Christ" (1 Thessalonians 5:23).

God wants us healed and whole. Jesus never once turned someone away who came to Him for healing. "Great crowds came to him, bringing the lame, the blind, the crippled, the mute and many others, and laid them at his feet; and he healed them (Matthew 15:30). And again it says in Luke 6:19, "The people all tried to touch him, because power was coming from him and healing them all."

Pastor Bill Johnson teaches that Jesus is perfect theology. Indeed, we can learn all about our heavenly Father through Jesus because "the Son is the image of the invisible God" (Colossians 1:15). God's heart is for us to walk in health physically, spiritually and emotionally. We know there is no sickness, tears or pain in heaven (Revelation 21:4), and Jesus taught us to pray "your kingdom come, your will be done, on earth as it is in heaven" (Matthew 6:10). God wants the very best for you!

1 Peter 2:24 tells us "'He himself bore our sins' in his body on the cross, so that we might die to sins and live for righteousness; 'by his wounds you have been healed.'" So God has already provided healing to us through what Jesus accomplished at Calvary. Now we must live into that provision. Through tapping, we appropriate His healing.

Bad habits, oftentimes, are tied to hurts we experienced years before. They are protective mechanisms we use, so we never get hurt again—or so we think. Often these protective behaviors get us into other immoral trouble, compounding our sin problem.

Prayer and Bible study help us to understand God's will for us. Knowledge alone is not enough to break down those old habits. We want to do better; we pledge to God to do better, but often we find ourselves falling back to our old ways.

This causes us more frustration, embarrassment, and anger, which we often direct at ourselves. Sometimes, we simply give up the struggle, knowing changes have never stuck in the past, so why bother trying to change now.

I've heard clients say that exact thing: "I can't seem to change. I'm so disgusted with myself."

EFT can be the tool God is handing you. Allow the Holy Spirit to point out what underpins the bad habits you have but cannot seem to break. According to the latest university research, these habits are literally stuck in your physiology As we tap, God breaks them down for you by discharging the emotion of the original trauma that lies underneath the behavior, bringing you into a closer relationship with Him. And that is the relationship most Christians desire so much—intimate communion with God.

Romans Chapter 8 shows us the Holy Spirit intercedes on our behalf, as stated in verses 26–27, "Likewise the Spirit helps us in our weakness. For we do not know what to pray for as we ought, but the Spirit himself intercedes for us with groanings too deep for words. And he who searches hearts knows what is the mind of the Spirit, because the Spirit intercedes for the saints according to the will of God."

He intercedes according to the will of God the Father, creator of all things, working everything together for our good (Romans 8:28). Verse 29 goes on to tell us believers, we were foreknown to share in the image of Christ, His Son, so we are justified, or saved by grace, destined for heaven where we will be glorified with Jesus before God's throne forever! EFT can be God's tool for us to press on in the image *(ikon)* of Christ, becoming sanctified as God calls us to be.

> Philippians 3:14 states Apostle Paul's goal, which he then gives to us: *"I press on toward the goal for the prize of the upward call of God in Christ Jesus."*

The Holy Spirit was Jesus' constant companion and friend, sustaining and guiding Him unto all things required by His Father. The Holy Spirit assisted Jesus to do the will of God right up and through His cruel death on the Cross at Calvary. Jesus submitted to the Holy Spirit's guidance and direction.

The Holy Spirit conceived Jesus, He matured Him, He sustained Him especially during satan's temptation in the wilderness (Matthew 4:1–11), He empowered

Christ through His three years of ministry on earth, He filled Jesus with His gifts, including holiness, He perfected Jesus right up until His death, and Jesus was raised from the dead on Easter morning by the power of the Holy Spirit (Romans 8:11).

Everything Jesus did was wrought by the power of the Holy Spirit (Acts 10:38). Because Jesus was fully man, He too was subject to every temptation visited upon you and me. Jesus resisted those temptations only through the prompting of the Holy Spirit, just as we are empowered to do today (Hebrews 4:15–16).

Jesus told us it was better that He go back to the Father in heaven so He could leave us in the hands of His Holy Spirit (John 14:15–31). In those verses, Jesus promises the Holy Spirit will teach us all things, testify of Christ, and guide us until the end of the world. The Holy Spirit uses the physiology God the Father created to help heal us. The Holy Spirit guides us toward that healing.

The Holy Spirit uses what our heavenly Father created to make us more like Jesus in all aspects of our lives, enhancing our spiritual life, and taking us forward to help others come to know Jesus as their Savior, as people witness our life being transformed by the Holy Spirit through the use of EFT.

We may have often echoed Apostle Paul's lament, "I have the desire to do what is good, but I cannot carry it out. For I do not do the good I want to do, but the evil I do not want to do—this I keep on doing" (Romans 7:18–19). As we tap, confess and repent, we physiologically remove from our mind and body many of the impediments to becoming more like Jesus. Tapping seems to work through our neurology to change habits in ourselves we so despise; those habits that do not exemplify Jesus in any manner, shape or form. As we tap, we often can more easily submit to the will of the Holy Spirit, allowing Him to remove bad habits and change us to become more and more like Christ.

Making the fruit of the Holy Spirit evident in our lives is an excellent indicator to determine to what degree we are abiding in the Vine, Who is Jesus (John 15:4–5). Using EFT often helps us allow the Holy Spirit to bring forth those fruit into our lives. As tapping usually leads us to forgiveness, love is manifested, and so are all the other gifts or fruit of the Holy Spirit as outlined in Galatians 5:22–23, "But the fruit of the Spirit is love, joy, peace, patience, kindness, goodness, faithfulness, gentleness, self-control; against such things there is no law."

God has handed us one of the most effective tools known to the modern Church –EFT!

CHAPTER 9

Sanctification

Jesus left the Holy Spirit here on earth after He ascended to heaven at the Resurrection (John 14:15–21). The Holy Spirit is our Helper. He helps us to live more Christ-like lives. It is the Holy Spirit who has the power to help us break bad habits to conform us more to the image of Christ.

However, we are responsible for and must participate in the process of sanctification. Salvation in Jesus Christ is free, but sanctification is our Christian work. We don't work for our salvation, but we are required to work to become more like Jesus in our behavior. We work out our soul's salvation with fear and trembling, at the same time realizing that it is actually God who is at work in us to will and do His good pleasure (Philippians 2:12–13).

To cooperate with His supernatural work in our hearts, we are encouraged to meditate on His Word, find a Bible believing church and attend worship regularly, associate with scripturally based Christian friends, find ourselves a Christian mentor or guide, and learn how to be a Godly Christian, acting on what we have learned through these teachings. This is the process of sanctification.

WHAT IS IT?

According to *Baker's Evangelical Dictionary of Biblical Theology*[62], "the generic meaning of sanctification is the state of proper functioning. In the theological sense, things are sanctified when they are used for the purpose God intends. A human being is sanctified, therefore, when he or she lives according to God's design and purpose."

---

62 Elwell, ed., *Evangelical Dictionary of Biblical Theology*, 1996.

Sanctification is translated in Greek as *hagiasmos*, which means "holiness." To sanctify, therefore, means "to make holy." The Greek word for someone who is a holy person is "saint" *(hagios)*, which is derived from the Greek word for sanctification. God commands that holiness in us, as stated in 1 Peter 1:15–16: "but as He who called you is holy, you also be holy in all your conduct, since it is written." Leviticus 19:2 states it like this: "You shall be holy, for I am holy."

> We are often called to that holiness as explained in 1 Peter 3:15–16, *"but in your hearts honor Christ the Lord as holy, always being prepared to make a defense to anyone who asks you for a reason for the hope that is in you; yet do it with gentleness and respect, having a good conscience, so that, when you are slandered, those who revile your good behavior in Christ may be put to shame."*

In the end analysis, we cannot sanctify ourselves as that is the work of the Holy Spirit. Our heavenly Father sanctifies us (1 Corinthians 1:30) by the Spirit (2 Thessalonians 2:13; 1 Peter 1:2) and in the name of Jesus, our Savior (1 Corinthians 6:11).

Trusting and obeying God is part of sanctification, but as Apostle Paul says in 2 Corinthians 7:1, "Since we have these promises, beloved, let us cleanse ourselves from every defilement of body and spirit, bringing holiness to completion in the fear of God," we are called to holiness and positive moral action.

"PARTICIPATING IN THE DIVINE NATURE"

Even though we were born with a sin nature due to Adam and Eve's disobedience in the Garden of Eden, we are still made in God's image. In fact, as regenerated Christians we have been born from above with an incorruptible seed, the DNA of God, and have a new divine nature (John 3:3; 1 Peter 1:23). "Therefore, if anyone is in Christ, the new creation has come: The old has gone, the new is here! (2 Corinthians 5:17). We have already been transformed on the inside; now we just need to release and live into that holiness. Peter describes what that looks like in his second epistle:

> *"His divine power has given us everything we need for a godly life through our knowledge of him who called us by his own glory and goodness. Through these he has given us his very great and precious promises, so that through them* ***you may participate in the divine nature,*** *having escaped the corruption in the world caused by evil desires. For this very reason, make every effort to add to your faith goodness; and to goodness, knowledge; and to knowledge,*

self-control; and to self-control, perseverance; and to perseverance, godliness; and to godliness, mutual affection; and to mutual affection, love. For if you possess these qualities in increasing measure, they will keep you from being ineffective and unproductive in your knowledge of our Lord Jesus Christ" (2 Peter 1:3–8, emphasis added by author).

James 3:9–10 speaks of how we are in God's image, but we act nothing like it! "With the tongue we praise our Lord and Father, and with it we curse men, who have been made in God's likeness. Out of the same mouth come praise and cursing. My brothers, this should not be."

Christ's redemptive power reversed in us all the moral ineptitude and disgrace. Because of this power, it is our responsibility to do our part in becoming more like Jesus—*"ikon,"* meaning the image of Christ. As He is, so also are we in this world (1 John 4:17).

Emotional Freedom Techniques can be a wonderful tool to help us become more like Christ. As we tap out our negative or immoral behaviors, we find our outer man conforming more closely to the holiness of our inner man, who has become the righteousness of God in Christ Jesus (2 Corinthians 5:21). Often immoral or socially bad behaviors are based in trauma, usually something someone did or said to us in childhood or young adulthood. Tapping usually works well to undo the emotional effects of those past events, leaving us the freedom to be like Jesus.

Apostle Paul writes in Romans 7:19, "For I do not do the good I want to do, but the evil I do not want to do—this I keep on doing." What sin or bad behavior are you plagued with that you vow to God again and again you will stop doing, but your resistance folds and once again you find yourself doing exactly what you vowed you'd never do again? Gambling? Overeating or gluttony? Fornication? Adultery? Theft? What's the sin issue in your life that you have prayed for God to remove? What behavior causes you intense shame because there in nothing you can do to break that bad habit?

WHY DO WE DO WHAT WE DO?

I bring good news—gospel—to you! EFT can be a wonderful tool that can remove obstacles from your life. Obstacles that are defensive and protective actions we keep repeating, trying to keep ourselves safe from events stuck in the lessons we learned in childhood. It's similar to the concept of "quitting a job before I get fired." We act out preemptively to avoid feeling or experiencing something we hate and that's awful. It is part of the process of what psychologists call "numbing out."[63]

We'll do just anything not to feel the rotten feelings that plague us. But how can we hear God's voice and what can we do when there are so many other critical "voices" talking in our head, telling us negative things about ourselves? We act out selfish, sinful behaviors to numb ourselves not to feel anything at all. These behaviors include drinking to excess, using street drugs, gambling, pornography, and overeating, which we do to soothe our feelings.

For example, did you know the reason you crave carbohydrates when you feel sad or anxious is physiological? Carbohydrates release the neurotransmitter dopamine, the pleasure chemical in our bodies. Once the carbohydrate high is gone, we crave more carbohydrates to get another boost of dopamine to make us feel terrific once again.

This is why so many people engage in thrill-seeking experiences like promiscuity and adultery. And they continue with their actions again and again, chasing the "high" associated with the pleasure chemicals released into their body. We desperately feel alone, abandoned due to some childhood issue, so what do we do now to avoid that feeling? We may go seeking sexual pleasure in all the wrong places. Underneath we fear having a stable adult relationship, and God forbid even consider marriage where our sexual pleasure is holy and encouraged, because the last stable person in our life, perhaps a parent, abandoned us, and we are certainly going to make sure that abandonment never happens again! When we cannot make our internal haunting feelings go away, we tend to look for ways to hide them, or seek ways to cover them up, or we simply try to forget they even exist.[64]

Are any of these thoughts conscious? They may not be. Your subconscious is so wonderfully constructed by God that it does all it can to protect you from future hurts. It will drive your life with one sole purpose—avoiding more of the same pain you once experienced. And sadly, that avoidance can lead you to separation from God because of the sin the avoidance leads you to do, thus causing increased bad feelings due to separation from God. The process, like many others, is cyclical and destructive.

By tapping away the emotions stored from early abandonment and isolation, God often clears the way for you to move into relationships far superior to anything

---

63   Van der Kolk, *The Body Keeps the Score*, 265–266.
64   Ibid., 120.

you can possibly imagine. And the tapping repairs the vertical relationship with God because now when you repent of your sin of fornication, you may stop the behavior, making it true repentance!

NO CONDEMNATION

While EFT is a fantastic tool to deal with all of the emotions we feel underneath the surface based on events from decades before, it also works well to deal with the condemnation heaped on us by our unhealed consciences and the evil one.

Satan enjoys his role in all of this. He loves to condemn us for our failures. Remember, the Holy Spirit convicts and reveals, but He does not condemn. "There is now no condemnation for those who are in Christ Jesus" (Romans 8:1). If you have confessed your transgression to God, but you still feel guilty about it, then it's not God speaking. That is satan! God remembers your sins no more once you have confessed them (Isaiah 43:25; Hebrews 8:12).

I've worked with several women in their 50's who had abortions 30 years ago. Their negative feelings run deep because they now understand they took the life of their unborn child. They saw the life inside them as an inconvenience then; they see it as a precious baby now.

It is extremely rare to run into one of these women who haven't confessed their sin of murdering her baby. Most of them express it in that exact manner. What baffles them most is why the guilt and remorse continue to have such a stinging, paralyzing impact on them.

Here again is where EFT can often excel at explaining the spiritual and physiological reasons why the emotional impact lingers decades later. The spiritual reason is that satan continues to condemn these women, even after they confessed their sin. He should never be listened to! Physiologically, their own emotional reactions around their abortions have been embedded and implanted within their cells. This is cellular memory.

> "Many of your attitudes, perceptions, and emotional responses are deeply ingrained in your cellular patterning. Your nerve cells store and retain accumulated memories of past and present emotionally charged events."[65]

---

65 Childre, *The HeartMathSolution*, 201–202.

Research seems to confirm the mind remembers much of what you have felt throughout your life, right down to the cellular level. So as these women listen to the feelings of their bodies, it reminds them of their abortions, with all its accompanying emotions, coming alive again with every part of their literal being. The women are actually reliving that abortion in their body and mind, triggering guilt or remorse in their spirit. With tapping, God can often change all of those reactions!

God completely changes your normal method of operating. Once your relationship with Him has been repaired through repentance, an often different and more peaceful feeling enters your heart. It did for me. The clouds of that sin lift, like the blinders Apostle Paul talked about in Acts 26:18, "to open their eyes and turn them from darkness to light, and from the power of Satan to God, so that they may receive forgiveness of sins and a place among those who are sanctified by faith." We walk in the light of Christ.

For myself and from what I have been told, the visual outside world suddenly looks differently after just a couple EFT sessions. The trees are greener, the sky is bluer, the details of a flower petal not noticed before suddenly stand out in amazing wonder. There is a seeing we have never experienced before. Life often begins to clarify itself. Things that once dominated our thinking no longer seem to matter. The emotional fog begins to lift and dissipate.

We've all heard stories of an alcoholic who has hung around bars for decades before coming to Jesus. Immediately, thereafter, he no longer hungers for alcoholic-type relationships, but ones that are more reflective of Who Jesus is. Tapping often does a similar thing. You will gravitate to happier, more joyful, more thankful Christians, people who know Jesus is their lifeblood.

I will warn you that many of your relationships might change once you grab onto God's EFT! It just happens. Some friends you've had for decades will simply fade away, but God will often bring in new people who are more in line with your new life in Christ. This type of change is the renewing of us into Christ-like behavior (2 Timothy 2:22–26; Romans 12:2; 2 Corinthians 5:17). This is similar to when you first became a Christian. Some people simply moved out of your life, but other believers moved into it.

This may also happen within your family. There will often be something "energetic" about it. You have fulfilled a particular place within your family structure since the day you were born. You filled some else's needs and they filled yours. Once

EFT begins to change your neurological and chemical make-up, those familial needs seem to change. Most often, they change for the better, so relationships either get stronger or simply fade away.

I've had mothers ask if I will tap with their troubled child. I have a standard answer in my EFT practice. "No, I will not tap with your son or daughter until you yourself spend time tapping with me. Children often reflect the behavior of their parents, particularly the mother. You must get your own emotional house in order before you can try to fix your children."

That same principle applies here. Relationships change, especially relationships with others with whom we may have had conflict for decades. When we forgive such a person, the animosity often drops out of that relationship and the glue that kept it together is gone. Therefore, the relationship simply falls apart, slipping away because the co-dependency seems to be gone.

This is change, but it is positive change! We can be grateful when the dynamics of our relationships change in such healthy, beneficial ways.

SUB-SECTION TWO:
The Mind-Spirit Gift for Healing

CHAPTER 10

Repent

Once we recognize our selfishness and the destructiveness of our sin, repentance can be ours. Repentance sheds the light of God's potential into our lives, the potential of living for Him into the glorious purposes and wonderful destinies He designed for us. "'For I know the plans I have for you,' declares the LORD, 'plans to prosper you and not to harm you, plans to give you hope and a future'" (Jeremiah 29:11).

To get there, we start where we are and just step up. Stepping up—taking responsibility for our lives, including the mistakes and sins we have made—is part of the correcting and cleansing process that often makes tapping effective. Little healing, either emotional or physical, can happen until we acknowledge we have a problem. When a doctor suggests a nutritional diet change for a patient, he cannot force the patient to eat a certain way. Not until the patient himself realizes and fully understands the need to implement the diet will he or she do so.

It is no different in our Christian walk. Until we realize we have need of a Savior, we continue on our merry way, doing life in whatever way we see fit. As that sinful life unravels before us, we begin to realize there must be a better way. This is where the Holy Spirit steps in convicting us, changing our minds, and turning us toward the Cross of Jesus Christ.

REPENTANCE DEFINED

"Repent" means "to change one's thinking," and it comes from the Greek *metanoia*, meaning "change of mind." Repentance is more than simply having the emotion of sorrow. Repenting is a verb, it is an action, a doing of something. True repentance requires a conscious decision to turn around our moral GPS—a "recalculating" of sorts—to change our mind about holding onto a habit, sin, negative feeling or thought, and choosing instead to give them to God.

This recalculation is a turning away from sin, selfishness, and rebellion and returning to the Lord with all of our mind, soul, and heart. It should happen often, whenever we realize something in our life is not of God. We want to align our thoughts with His thoughts, experiencing the mind of Christ (1 Corinthians 2:16). We want to align our emotions with His emotions, experiencing the fruit of His Holy Spirit—love, joy and peace (Galatians 5:22).

We were born selfish. Does an infant consider the fact that her parents just may need a good night's sleep when she awakens hungry and wet at 3 A.M? Absolutely not! That child feels her physical discomfort and the bawling begins, promptly and loudly.

As adults we often haven't progressed much further than that 3-month-old baby in our Christian walk. I know I hadn't. Because of my deeply damaged emotional state, all I thought about was how badly I hurt inside. My behavior reflected my own internal torment. I wasn't a very pleasant person to be around. Nothing in life seemed to be worth living for, and I had been a born-again Christian for more than 30 years!

As I was taught as a child, I confessed and repented of the wrong things I did, but it never dawned on me how I *felt* was just as sinful. My emotions and thoughts around negative life events and the people who perpetrated them against me were antithesis to who I was as a Christian. I was so blinded I couldn't see that. Well, God dropped Emotional Freedom Techniques into my life and all of that changed, very abruptly!

EVIL EMOTIONS?

Many of our emotions are at times sinful. It's that plain and that simple. Consider this list: aggravation, anger, fear, frustration, resentment, distrust, self-pity, and the one I consider the most insidious—shame.

Of course, thousands of different emotions and their variations abound, but this short list has nothing positive about it. All of these self-righteous emotions lead us straight into the pit of self-absorption. We are the center of our own world, which is a complete contradiction to what God expects of us! This is a direct violation of the First Commandment. God can't come first in our lives. We are our own god.

He is to be our delight and the center of our being, not ourselves. This is exactly what got Adam and Eve in trouble in the Garden of Eden. They wanted to be equal to God, when the serpent spun his tale about what God said regarding the Tree of Knowledge.

Our sinful nature, inherited from our first parents, is still alive and well in our hearts—until we repent and confess that attitude, reforming and turning our lives around to reflect the Glory of God, and Who He really is.

Matthew 16:25 promises, "For whoever wants to save their life will lose it, but whoever loses their life for Me will find it." It is that letting go of our selfish will, submitting it to the will of the Father as Jesus did, that finally gives us that lasting joy and peace we all so desperately crave in this harried world.

It is our responsibility to come to repentance with the help of the Holy Spirit. He is the One who gently reveals where we are out of sync with the Father, and empowers us to live righteously and reign in life through Jesus (Romans 5:17).

1 John 1:9 declares, "If we confess our sins, then He is faithful and just to forgive our sins." You can't confess until you realize the need to do so. That's repentance! We see the error of our ways as something blocking our walk with God and His best for us, and we adjust our thinking. We change our mind and agree with God about that behavior.

Confession then follows as we take responsibility and ownership of all those actions and negative emotions and thoughts, choosing to rid ourselves of them permanently. "I acknowledged my sin to You and did not cover up my iniquity. I said I will confess my transgressions to the Lord, and You forgave the guilt of my sins" (Psalm 32:5).

God then changes these thoughts and emotions, realigning them with His thoughts. He seems to have given us EFT to help us along with this job through the physiology He created in us. Often, hurts can then heal, and we can allow forgiveness to reign in our lives, freeing us of that burden. "Repent then and turn to God so that your sins may be wiped out, that times of refreshing may come down from the Lord" (Acts 3:19).

EXPERIENCING GOD

As we tap away our deep emotional pain, God comes alive in our hearts and minds. This often is one of the outstanding gifts of EFT. I hear this routinely from those who have done a thorough job of tapping. They begin to *feel* God in their lives. He was always there, but the muck and mire of their emotional life hid Him from them. Now, they experience His presence!

We can then begin every day afresh because He has washed us clean in the blood of the precious Savior. Psalm 51 reads, "Create in me a clean heart, Oh God, and renew a right spirit with me. Restore to me the joy of Your salvation and uphold me with Your free Spirit." Where is this restoration of joy found? With God. "You make known to me the path of life; you will fill me with joy in your presence, with eternal pleasures at your right hand." He wants us living in that place of holy joy and pleasure. God cares about our feelings. He wants the very best for us!

HOW SIN STEALS JOY

Most sin is repetitive. We do the same thing again and again, in spite of our best efforts to reform. In Romans 7:14–23 Apostle Paul describes it this way:

> *"We know that the law is spiritual, whereas I am weak flesh sold into the slavery of sin. I cannot even understand my own actions. I do not do what I want to do but what I hate. When I act against my own will, by that very fact I agree that the law is good. This indicates that it is not I who do it but sin which resides in me. I know that no good dwells in me, that is, my flesh; the desire to do right is there but not the power. What happens is that I do, not the good I will to do, but the evil I do not intend. But if I do what is against my will, it is not I who do it, but sin which dwells in me. This means that even though I want to do what is right, a law that leads to wrongdoing is always ready at hand. My inner self agrees with the law of God, but I see in my body's members another law at war with the law of my mind; this makes me the prisoner of the law of sin in my members."*

It's as if we cannot help ourselves. We also get tired or feel guilty if we repetitively repent of the same sin time and again. Perhaps we feel we are cheapening the blood of Christ if we say it one more time, so we hesitate to tell God again we are sorry for the repeated sin. We feel terrible, but we still don't confess and enjoy a clean conscience.

Remember that David tells us in Psalm 103:12, He removes our sins, "As far as the east is from the west so far has He put our transgressions from us." And verse 3 of that Psalm tells us, "He pardons all your iniquities; He heals all your ills." In reality, God hears our prayer anew each time we repent, even if it's the same old sad story.

While some Christians fixate on their failings and suffer from desperation and despair because they cannot reform in spite of their very best effort, other Christians feel no conviction of sin. They say they believe in the redeeming blood of Jesus, but they just go on their merry way, never thinking of sin or its consequences.

Lee Strobel wrote, "Few things accelerate the peace process as much as humbly admitting our own wrongdoing and asking for God's forgiveness." Repentance, the changing of our thinking to God's thinking, is first. For a Christian, confession of sins is second. We need to acknowledge our shortcomings before God.

Therefore, it's easy to see how significant repentance and confession are within Christian EFT. Many of our emotions are based in sin. We are so busy feeling the emotions that we have no time to truly consider what these sinful feelings do to us, spiritually as well as physically. We now know everything we think and feel impacts the health of our body. Our sin also impacts our health. As sinful emotions are carried to different cells of our body, they cause us stress, damaging the cells involved, which causes their eventual death, which causes disease.

Jesus' death on the cross at Calvary atoned for that sin, making us right with God once again, but it is our responsibility to maintain that right relationship through regular repentance and confession of our sins, thereby aiding the maintenance of our good physical health.

Many of us are familiar with the acronym A.C.T.S. as a model for prayer: adoration, confession, thanksgiving and supplication. We often forget the first three components and get right to the asking! We should always remember the correct order of prayer: praise, repentance and confession, thanksgiving for blessings received, and then, finally, at the end, we can dive into the favor-asking. Once we have our hearts and minds in agreement with God's heart and mind, we'll be pleasantly surprised at how quickly His answers to our prayers readily manifest!

Personally, I teach and advocate that Christian EFTers tap while praying.

We seem to know now that tapping drops us into lower brainwave states (alpha and theta), as does praying in tongues, as Charity so states. Even though I have no scientific proof of this, I truly believe that those lower brainwave states open us up to hearing God's voice more clearly.

Experiment with prayer and tapping together. Let me hear your thoughts on this subject at EFTforChristians@gmail.com.

CHAPTER 11

Confess

Emotional Freedom Techniques often works best when we tap about specific memories or events—and so does confession. We tell God what we did wrong, taking responsibility for all of it. Confession means, "saying the same thing as," i.e., to agree with or concede to. Sin means to "miss the mark." So when we confess our sin, we're saying or agreeing with the exact thing God says about our behavior—we are agreeing with Him that we have missed the mark.

While tapping, we ask Holy Spirit to search our heart and highlight exactly what happened to us—from which event or memory does He want to release us. We "agree" with what He reveals by confessing every aspect or emotion of that remembered event. Although the subconscious employs dissociation to hide events and their details from us, tapping while we pray helps to unlock those hidden memories. The thoughts in our hearts are like deep water, but we draw them out with understanding (Proverbs 20:5).

Holy Spirit's river within us also runs deep, since it's out of our *innermost* being that His living water flows (John 7:37–39). EFT is a tool that allows us to connect with this river of life. Jesus doesn't live in our heads; He lives in our hearts (Ephesians 3:17). Through tapping, we are able to more effortlessly shift down into our spirits, which are joined to His Spirit (1 Corinthians 6:17).

It seems as we lower our brainwaves into alpha range, added detail around an event and its sinful part emerges. This empowers us to confess the sin more fully, shining the Light of God's truth into that dark space in our hearts. "The spirit of man is the lamp of the Lord, searching all the innermost parts of his being" (Proverbs 20:27).

We surrender this sin at the foot of the cross where it belongs because Jesus already died and paid the eternal price for our sin. Tapping often allows us to *feel* the release of this surrender and experience the freedom it brings. We are able to walk away from the sinful thought, feeling or habit, which allows the Lord to not only change our minds around the habit, but sometimes the physiology, too. In a very tangible way, He is supernaturally transforming us into His image (Romans 8:29). God is working in us to will and do His good pleasure, until Christ is fully formed in us (Philippians 2:13; Galatians 4:19).

Once we see the extent of the problem, we tap and confess the consequences of the sinful habit and its associated emotions. Sometimes, consequences include additional sins that accompany the event. Typically, we discover more than one sin within any given event. One thing leads to another. Some of the sins are actions; others are thoughts around those actions; and still others are the accompanying feelings during and following those actions or thoughts.

Invite the Holy Spirit to reveal everything involved with a specific sin and confess it all while tapping. Tapping can clear out the emotions accompanying our sin and seems to prevent the emotions from lodging within our cellular receptors, which causes them to die. We want to root out all this negativity from our cells immediately before the physical damage is done.

MEMORY'S WINDOW

Once we access a memory, we have a window of several hours to change that memory. Memories change with each and every re-telling. This process is called "memory reconsolidation." While tapping, we are also going for "memory extinction," whereby, the emotional charge is pulled out of the memory. Dr. Joe Dispenza teaches that "A memory without the emotional charge is wisdom."[66]

Bruce Ecker, with Joseph E. Le Doux, has done much scientific work in the area of "memory reconsolidation."[67] One of Mr. Ecker's premises, as he states in the previously cited YouTube video, is that in childhood we learn many things that are implicit, subconscious thoughts of which we are unaware that run our lives as core beliefs. The root cause of most of our unwanted, negative behaviors is this piece of emotional implicit learning. Bruce explains how the synaptic connection to these implicit memories become labile for several hours, allowing us an

---

66   www.drjoedispenza.com/blog/general/creating-lasting-change/
67   If you are interested in watching one of his YouTube talks, please visit www.youtube.com/watch?v=_V_rl2N6Fco.

opportunity to neurally rewire and change a lifelong negative belief to a positive God-honoring one.[68]

In his book, *Life Together*[69], Reverend Dietrich Bonhoeffer asks why it appears to be easier to confess our sins to God than to a brother or sister in Christ. Since our brother or sister is imperfect as we are, it should be easier to confess to them than to confess to our holy God. It is easier to confess our sins to God because we are actually just confessing it all to ourselves and we then just grant ourselves absolution. He goes on to postulate this may be one of the reasons for our relapsing into sin, leaving our obedience weak and unstable. We Christians focus on a life based on "living on self-forgiveness and not a real forgiveness."

Bonhoeffer continues to say God gave us communion with one another so we may avail ourselves of confessing to our brother or sister so as to not allow us to remain alone, afraid, and isolated in our sins, so the darkness of our sin can be brought to the Light of Jesus.

This socialization factor is interesting in light of a relatively new neuroscience theory by Dr. Steven Porges called the "Polyvagal Theory"[70]. Dr. Porges postulates via a rather complex physiological method that much of our emotional angst comes when the socialization aspect of our life is harmed or warped.

Confession of sin pulls open the heavy closet door that often hides all our relational issues, allowing Christ's Light of the Gospel in, exposing the sin, setting us free so these sins no longer have any hold over us. Our sin locks us up inside ourselves, alone and isolated from fellowship with other Christians and from enjoying communion with our God. Sin maintains a very selfish lifestyle within us. Sin is embarrassing, making us keep a safe distance from everyone, including God, in the hope no one notices our sinful deficiencies.

LIVING LIGHT

Sin is controlling, but it breaks easily when it is exposed to Jesus' Light as John 8:12 states, "I am the Light of the world. No follower of mine shall ever walk in darkness; no, he shall possess the Light of life." In fact, we are light ourselves! "For you were formerly darkness, but now you are Light in the Lord; walk as children of Light, (for the fruit of the Light consists in all goodness and righteousness and truth), trying to learn what is pleasing to the Lord" (Ephesians 5:8–10).

---

68 Ecker, *Unlocking the Emotional Brain*, 2012.
69 Bonhoeffer, *Life Together*, 2009.
70 www.stephenporges.com/

Tapping can help us let our inner Light of Christ shine through. It can break down those sinful habits because we allow Jesus to eliminate the basis of why we feel or do harmful actions. Underneath every "bad" habit a trauma—whether big or small—often lurks. You act on those behaviors for a specific purpose or reason. Often those reasons are defensive in nature. You act to ward off or negate the behaviors of others toward you.

For example, your mother berated you as a child every time you failed to come home with all A's and B's on your report card. This went on your entire childhood. You never felt you were worthy enough or good enough to accomplish anything in school no matter how hard you tried or how much your mom wished. These defeating attitudes of your mother's are now seared into every cell of your body, you can still hear her exact words and her mannerisms as she said the words to you.

Now, as an adult, like in the story of AgnesMary in Chapter Three, you will do anything in your life to avoid criticism. AgnesMary internalized her fear of criticism, raising her blood pressure. But, perhaps, you externalize your fear. Every time your boss approaches your desk with a stride that reminds you of your mother's critical attitude toward you, you lash out at the boss, cutting him off before he can launch into his diatribe, or so you think, about what you are doing wrong in the office.

The boss is kind, and he assumes you are just having a bad day, allows you to diffuse your anger on him, as you spout off to him that you are doing your best and he should just back off and leave you alone. This is anger at your mother for her demeaning attitude toward you 35 years ago. You perceived what you thought the boss was thinking based on your memories of how your mom treated you. Sadly, in reality, your boss only wanted to invite you to the Friday evening party at his house in honor of his wife's 50th birthday.

You refuse to attend the party because you are now embarrassed about the way you just treated him. In reality, this conversation wasn't about either of you—it was about your mother's treatment of you when you were a grade-school child.

Here is where Dr. Porges' Polyvagal Theory comes into effect. Your cranial nerves (vagal) system is possibly damaged because of earlier trauma from your mother, and because of it you now have a skewed social sense, always misinterpreting the behavior of others toward you.[71]

---

71 Van der Kolk, *The Body Keeps the Score*, 78.

Here could be an excellent place to insert EFT into your life. Your mother harmed your emotions when you were a child and your neurology absorbed and cemented those attitudes in place within your body-mind. You react to any situation that now reminds you of mother's attitude toward you by lashing out before another human being hurts you. But by applying tapping to those memories, you can disconnect your mom's attitude from your physiology, freeing you to now resume life as a responsible, more content adult, rather than acting as the self-centered child you once were.

As you tap and confess your sin around that long-buried anger toward your mother, God will forgive your sin, but He also will loosen the behavior around the sin, possibly giving you a freedom you always wanted to live as a child of God.

Confession is therapeutic, in the best sense of the word. James 1:16a instructs us to confess to a confidante, "Hence, declare your sins to one another, and pray for one another, that you may find healing." Healing. That can be what you get when you tap. Spiritual, mental, emotional, and physical healing, like James wrote, is often what Christian EFT offers you.

Jesus already knows all our sins, but we must acknowledge them in order to obtain forgiveness and release from their consequences. Sin disrupts our fellowship with our Creator. The Christian who practices confession in her life is the one whom you trust to confess to because she understands the importance and the sacredness of the process. Remember always that forgiveness of our sin has absolutely nothing to do with us, or whether or not we feel we deserve forgiveness. It is all dependent on the already-completed work of Jesus at Calvary.

We were created to live in intimate fellowship with God as His beloved children. Sin comes between us and our heavenly Father, but only until we confess it. Once confessed, it is immediately forgiven! We see the gift of confession and freedom it brings by restoring us into a peaceful relationship with God and with ourselves once again.

SCIENCE OF CONFESSION

In his book, *How to Stop the Pain*, Dr. Jim Richards writes:

> "Guilt calls for punishment. When we feel guilt or shame, we have a need to be punished – so every cell in our bodies works to bring about our beliefs… If we believe we have done something that deserves physi-

cal punishment, we will have pain and sickness… Confession is the only thing that frees us from the expectation of judgment."[72]

Confession of sin is one of the key components missing today in the life of modern Christians. I find it invaluable when accompanied by EFT! It causes us to go inside ourselves. This mindfulness and introspection is what can heal both our minds and bodies by ridding them of all our piled-on sins and negative emotions we learned over years.

In addition to the memorized negative emotions, we also usually have a life of failed actions because of the paralysis caused by the early-in-life traumas, feelings, and lack of forgiveness. These add yet another basketful of emotions such as regret, remorse, grief, anger, and un-forgiveness towards others. God is faithful to create in us a new heart and spirit if we simply repent by recognizing that these emotions are causing us problems, and then confessing them for what they are— sins against God, others, and ourselves.

> *"The precepts of the LORD are right, giving joy to the heart. The commands of the LORD are radiant, giving light to the eyes. The fear of the LORD is pure, enduring forever. The ordinances of the LORD are sure and altogether righteous. They are more precious than gold, than much pure gold; they are sweeter than honey, than honey from the comb. By them is your servant warned; in keeping them there is great reward"* (Psalm 19:8–11).

God gave us the gifts of EFT and the physiology that responds to it. Because He created this self-healing mechanism within our physiology, we should avail ourselves of it to help us break through these sin barriers. As we repent and confess our faults more fully to the Lord, in exchange we receive a new desire to live for our God, serving both Him and others.

As a practitioner, I use confession as part of my EFT tapping, and you can do the same for yourself or for those with whom you also tap. As the client expresses all the different emotions involved around an event, I simply ask them the question, "Have you confessed this emotion?" If the answer is a resounding "yes," then we simply continue to tap. If the answer is "no," I inquire if the client wants me to lead a prayer of confession. To date, I have yet to have anyone refuse to do so, and clients always seem grateful we did.

---

72 Richards, *How to Stop the Pain*, 151, 161–162.

EFT and confession are powerfully anointed tools to realign us with our Father's heart and restore the joy of our salvation (Psalm 51:12). Jesus taught us the Kingdom of Heaven is within (John 17:21). It is a Kingdom of joy and peace, and tapping seems to be one of the simplest ways to live there (Romans 14:17).

THE POWER OF CONFESSION BY CHARITY KAYEMBE

My family and friends know I am a very positive, peppy, perky Pollyanna most all of the time. The glass is always half full, and I easily see every silver lining in any situation. That is, except, when I'm tapping.

If you were to eavesdrop while I tap, you would be shocked. The words coming out of my mouth most of the time that I'm tapping are evil, ungodly and sinful. And that's what I want. That's how it should be because I use tapping as my confession.

First John 1:9 declares, "If we confess our sins, then He is faithful and just to forgive our sins." IF we confess. So if I'm stewing emotionally, simmering in negative feelings, but I don't confess them, they can't be forgiven. We have to first admit there is sin if we want the blood of Jesus to cleanse us from all unrighteousness. We are not encouraging or endorsing the unrighteous thought or feeling; we are freeing ourselves of it.

When we confess our sin to God, it should sound bad. It *is* bad. We need to identify the evil thoughts in our mind and acknowledge the sinful emotions in our heart. We call sin out for what it is. I am not my thoughts and feelings, so I identify, separate and remove the negative thoughts and feelings from me.

Consequently when I'm ticked off, I tap negative. I tap mean and nasty. Now, I don't actually know very many bad words, so that aspect doesn't last long. But I keep going! I say every single hurtful, hateful thing I can think of regarding that specific situation, person or event.

When I'm in a place of emotional pain or offense, I naturally want revenge. But I don't just want to live naturally, but supernaturally. So I tap, and I tap the carnal, fleshly thoughts and emotions out. I tap them off and out of and away from me. And then they're gone. They are not in me anymore.

The process can take as little as thirty seconds because I tap often enough that tension doesn't build. I have become sensitive to my spirit and want to protect it. I watch over my heart with all diligence because I know the springs of life flow from it (Proverbs 4:23). So if I feel any stress, sadness, overwhelm, frustration, disappointment, anger or negativity whatsoever, I tap.

I'm well aware that out of the abundance of my heart, the mouth speaks (Luke 6:45). So if all of this garbage is coming out of my mouth, what does that say about my heart? Well, I'm tapping while I'm yapping, so I am cleaning house. I'm purifying my heart.

Jeremiah 4:14 reveals that evil thoughts can lodge within us. Ecclesiastes 7:9 warns that anger rests in the heart of fools. So I don't want these evil thoughts and feelings to get too comfortable within me. I'm kicking them out before they can make themselves at home in my heart and in my cellular memory.

I find the alternative to openly confessing my sins freely before my God to be much worse. That alternative is living in denial, trying to stuff the feelings or ignore them and pretend they're not there.

KEEPING IT REAL

God likes it when we keep it real. King David was a man after God's own heart, and he said some pretty terrible things about what he wanted God to do to his enemies. He confessed to God that he wanted Him to break their arm (Psalm 10:15); shatter their teeth (Psalm 58:6); and consume them in His wrath (Psalm 59:13). All kinds of stuff I hadn't even thought before!

You'll notice David's emotional outbursts didn't seem to faze God, though. So they shouldn't faze us either. In the same way we understand that a grumpy three-year-old doesn't really "hate" us, regardless of what his overtired complaints may be, God gets it. He knows our hearts and how we feel whether we admit to those feelings or not.

God cannot remove those feelings or heal us of emotions until we admit and acknowledge we have them, which we do through our confession. And tapping into our deepest emotions can make our repentance, confession and subsequent healing go deeper.

> So I use EFT as my confession: "*God, I confess I feel all these sinful emotions. God, I confess that I have all these evil thoughts. So, here You go. I'm tapping them out of my mind and tapping them out of my heart and surrendering them to You. I'm not entertaining those thoughts. I'm not engaging those emotions. I'm giving them to You. I'm done with them now.*"

We must tap whatever feels true to us in the moment. I always tap anything bad, as soon as it crosses my mind. Immediately upon a negative thought entering my consciousness or a bad feeling creeping in, I tap on it.

A principle of dream interpretation is we have to be "for real." If we are disingenuous in any way, then it won't work. And so it is with EFT. We have to be completely honest about what we are thinking and feeling, or else we won't get anywhere. When we can observe our thoughts and feelings, realize they are separate from us and not actually who we are, then we're making progress. We can then be empowered by the realization that this negativity can simply be tapped away.

WHAT THIS LOOKS LIKE

I'll share an example of how this could work in real life. Let's say someone on the phone is incredibly rude, demanding and disrespectful when she calls our office. She doesn't know me, but I'm trying to help her, even though she is difficult and unpleasant to communicate with in every way.

I hang up the phone and logically understand this caller's attitude has nothing to do with me. Obviously, this is a broken person, living in extreme dysfunction. The way she acted is merely a reflection on her, not me. I need to have the right perception about this situation and not take anything said to me during that conversation personally.

Well, that's nice, and it's certainly the mature Christ-like thing to do. However, I've just been verbally assaulted. How dare the caller say that to me! I know by memory Scriptures about love covering a multitude of sin, and how I need to forgive those thoughtless remarks. Those are great verses, but I'm not there. I'm not feeling them. Love is a feeling; forgiveness involves my emotions. And as much as I know I need to be walking in grace, in that moment, I'm just not.

So I tap. And I confess to God how thoroughly disgusted and offended I am with this caller. It's His child after all, so maybe I'll be mad at God about this, too! Where was He during that call anyway? Why doesn't He protect me from all the mean people who say unkind things?

Granted, it wasn't the end of the world, but for a moment in time, it felt like a pretty big deal.

Less than a minute later, I'm tapped out. It's over! And I move on. The negativity has been *acknowledged*. It's been *confessed*. It is not ignored; it is not denied; it is not lodged in my heart and buried in my cellular memory, so it can turn up as cancer in 20 years.

The cumulative effect of disregarding unholy feelings day after day is they become internalized and can manifest as degenerative disease down the road. For example, my father experienced arthritis in his knee and fingers as a direct result of his unprocessed emotions. His painful joints were completely restored to health upon extending heartfelt forgiveness through inner healing prayer.

This is why it's so important that we deal with negativity immediately and tap it away, so it is no longer part of our lives. It is gone because we confessed it in a way we could feel. Now those sinful thoughts and evil emotions are not only spiritually removed from us, they are physically removed, too.

THE BREAKTHROUGH: SEEING SIN FOR WHAT IT IS

That is the reason why we want emotions like fear and thoughts like worry to be understood for the sins that they are. It is not condemnation; it is freedom! We don't want you to be afraid, and then add guilt on top of your fears and worries. Not at all. The point is wrong thoughts and feelings are sinful, and Jesus has set us free from sin! We don't have to be slaves to fear and anxiety anymore. That's what the cross was about: freedom.

We create a problem when we don't identify wrong thoughts as sin and when we don't identify ungodly emotions as sin, instead we simply wallow in them. We continue to bathe our cellular receptors in the sin of anxiety. Biochemically, we're sinning. Against ourselves! We think the thoughts that fuel the neurochemistry that releases the peptides and hormones that steep our physical cells in toxic chemicals. And then we say a two-second "prayer" of certain words and call our confession good enough. Really?

Obviously, what many of us have been doing is not working. We have just as many Christians struggling with fear and worry as unbelievers. We have just as many believers as non-believers suffering from the physical ramifications of extended periods of increased cortisol levels—all manner of degenerative disease. This is unacceptable and it is not the abundant life for which Christ died. Maybe it's time we try something different. Maybe it's time we try EFT.

CHAPTER 12

Forgive

As a Christian EFT practitioner, I know repentance and confession of sins are important parts of the EFT process. Within that confession and repentance is often found forgiveness, which is an integral part of Emotional Freedom Techniques—particularly in Christian EFT. By forgiving ourselves and forgiving others, we free ourselves from the toxic internal emotional environment in which we have been living.

After repairing the vertical relationship with our heavenly Father via our repentance, EFT often brings in forgiveness, which repairs the horizontal relationships here on earth as well. We want God to forgive us, but we, too, must be willing to forgive others (Matthew 6:14–15).

MARIA'S STORY – LONG-TERM ANXIETY DISORDER

I was in desperation, seeking relief from 7 continuous years of physician diagnosed "general anxiety disorder," when I believe the Lord directed me to EFT. I had learned of EFT in 2005, but hadn't paid much attention to the healing powers of its use. Long-term anxiety is very debilitating and virtually controls one's life—and mine had spun out of my control, both day and night. In fact, I dreaded going to bed at night because of the night sweats, racing heart, middle of the night panic attacks, and constant disrupted sleep pattern. I was bone tired yet shuddered when facing the cycle of terrible nights, awaking with chatter in my head, nausea, and then fearing another depressing day.

In my prayers and internet research for a Christian EFT practitioner, I found several; however, the Lord kept directing me back to Sherrie Rice Smith. I contacted Sherrie and we set up a free consult, which led to me making a series of appointments directed at relieving my anxiety. First we tapped generally on anxiety for a few minutes so my body could calm down. I felt much calmer, my stomach quit churning and my shaking eased.

As we tapped on my triggers, we dug deeper and deeper into the root core issues of my fears. The first fears were of me being alone, which had many aspects. Being riddled with long-term daily anxiety, I was both tired and wired, meaning my body was not able to relax and in a constant state of flight. The slightest thing would trigger stress-producing cortisol and send my taxed adrenals into overdrive. Tapping helped calm my body immediately. I remember after each of the first few sessions of tapping I would go take a nap—what a sweet relief for my tired body and mind. EFT calmed me enough to sleep!

Before I first started tapping, I was not able to stay home alone for a whole day. I was so consumed with anxiety that I hated being alone and had to move about all the time. It is a very complex situation because I was so tired, yet compulsively agitated and wired.

My mind was cluttered and scattered, leaving me chronically tired and depressed. Sherrie told me the chatter and unwanted thoughts in my head would eventually go away. Oh how I longed for that, as each morning I dreaded waking up to unwanted thoughts. I know this sounds slightly crazy, but it was very real. No matter how much I willed them away or tried to take my thoughts captive they would resurface.

There was some skepticism on my part that this would actually work. We did not tap specifically on the thoughts in my head, instead focusing on core the issues that were the cause of these thoughts. Much to my amazement and relief, I now wake up with a clear head. After a couple of tapping sessions, I was not so wired and able to stay home and concentrate better. In my part-time job I was much more focused and able to get my work done efficiently. My hands were no longer shaking and my feet were no longer tapping all the time.

As an adult child of an alcoholic home, I can now see there was much trauma in my growing up years. This trauma instilled many triggers into my subconscious, which played into my fight, flight, and freeze responses. In my late 20's and early 30's, I experienced the sudden death of two significant loved ones in my life, thus more trauma, resulting in greater anxiety. As we tapped I realized how much forgiveness work I yet had to do. I knew I had to forgive, but that pain was bound up tightly within those deaths and all the circumstances I was left to deal with alone with two small children.

Sherrie gently led me through releasing the anxiety and triggers in each trauma. Some of my anxiety was rooted in being left behind, being left alone, rejection as a child, even though it was not intentional on my parents part, that was my perception. We tapped on a multitude of core issues bringing relief and clearing those triggers out of my mind. After each tapping session I was very tired. At first I was not sure how much healing was taking place, but over the following days permanent relief around the presenting issues remained stable and dissipated even further.

After several sessions I was able to sleep more soundly at night because, as my cortisol levels diminished, my adrenals were able to heal, which meant my body no longer was subject to those nighttime triggers. In long-term "generalized anxiety," I don't believe it is a one-time quick fix as there are many presenting issues that need to be addressed. EFT definitely calmed my body and mind beginning with the very first session. I kept tapping on each specific trigger in subsequent sessions. It's amazing how I felt more and more relaxed and able to cope as the days and weeks went by.

In each session the anxiety symptoms diminished as the triggers around that specific core issue were released. Considering I had 58 years of trauma stored up in my mind and body, it took a number of sessions to completely annihilate my anxiety symptoms. I now better comprehend how the body bears the burdens of many years of trauma. Today, with continued tapping as well as proper nutritional support, I know I will never experience such debilitating anxiety again.

I am so grateful for EFT because all of the other modalities I tried were unsuccessful in "permanently" disabling the triggers in my mind that caused my anxiety that was underneath my lack of forgiveness. Amazingly, the process only took a few months, and I know without a doubt EFT has cleared my traumas. I no longer dwell on them or even remember some of them. The ones I do remember no longer hold an emotional charge for me, what blessed relief!

The unwanted thoughts in my head, heart palpitations, night sweats, nausea, sleepless nights, chronic fatigue, shaking, many aches and pains, fear of being alone, fear of rejection, judgment from others…are all gone, and have been

> *replaced with a sense of abilities of mine that have resurfaced after having been long buried. EFT has given me so much hope for the rest of my life. Freedom is sweet! Through EFT there is hope and help for those suffering with long-term generalized anxiety.*
>
> *As a Christian, I know where my healing has come from—my Lord God. He is our Healer! I thank Him daily for leading me to Christian EFT. To Him goes all the praise and glory for this life-changing skill!*

As a result of her own experience in using this powerful healing modality, Maria Ellings is now pursuing a path as a Certified EFT practitioner.[73] Her story was presented here in her own words. There are no guarantees you will achieve these same results; this testimony is Maria's personal experience using Christian EFT.

BIOLOGY OF UNFORGIVENESS

Scripture instructs us time and again to forgive one another. Unforgiveness is anger that is purposeful, malignant, vengeful, and often retaliatory. It emotionally drains us on a minute-by-minute basis. Unforgiveness and anger can kill us if we harbor it long enough.

The lack of forgiveness in our life is a huge stressor to our bodies, one of the largest we can carry. Unforgiveness is wrapped up in so many different negative emotions, and each of the chemicals it produces courses through our bodies like waves washing over us on an ocean beach. They seem to never end.

Unforgiveness taxes your immune system, allowing diseases and illnesses to creep in, possibly destroying one's health. Unforgiveness drives your cortisol level—the metabolism regulating hormone—ever higher, reducing the available amount of much needed DHEA you need to rest and revive cells in your body.

Eventually, lack of forgiveness can lead to depression. Therefore, it is imperative we allow God to lead us to forgive, but how do we do that when we're so deeply hurt?

EFT will usually eventually lead us to forgiveness—IF we have continued tapping with due diligence. Therefore, once we learn to tap, we must steadily tap daily during our devotional and prayer times and at times when we need to seriously

---

73 www.tappingchristianeft.com

tap about a specific event or emotional memory, or an immediate trigger, as Charity's example in the previous chapter showed.

The fire safety adage is, "Drop and roll!" EFT adage is, "Stop and tap!" whenever a trigger appears, or at least at minimum, write down the trigger in order that you can tap on it later when time allows.

Jackie Viramontez, a Christian Practitioner in Los Angeles, recounts the story, which follows shortly, to illustrate how God brings in self-forgiveness once we tap away the sensory input and thoughts around how we feel about a tragic accident. Sometimes our angst is more about how we feel about ourselves than how we feel toward others.

We are told clearly in Scripture to "Love your neighbor as yourself" (Mark 12:31). If we have no compassion for ourselves, why would we have compassion and love for those around us? Our family, friends, and neighbors are extensions of ourselves. When Jesus told His disciples to love their neighbor, He meant for them to love themselves equally!

Children and young adults tend to clear their issues quickly because they aren't carrying around decades of emotional baggage. Forgiveness, therefore, can sometimes happen in one session; other times, it simply takes longer to achieve. Persistence in using EFT is often the key.

Jackie Viromontez wrote this next case study with a lot of detail, and I have included it here as it was written to give you an understanding of the flow and sequence of a real-time tapping session with a certified practitioner.

CASE STUDY

Kristina, aged 27, came to me because she was suffering from stress symptoms from an accident that occurred three months prior. She had been hit by a car while crossing the street. Her leg had been broken in a few places, and although she was physically healing, she was in need of emotional support.

Her cast was off, and she was pushing herself to drive and walk around on the street where the accident occurred. Although she did not feel afraid of the cars, drivers, or traffic sounds, she would break down in tears if a horn went off, or if she stood at the edge of a cross walk. Her mind told her she was safe, but her body responded otherwise. She knew it was her fight or flight response trying to protect her, but she didn't know how to tell her brain that she was safe.

She had heard about my work from a friend at our church, and decided to schedule a session. I asked her how she felt about the accident, and tears filled her eyes. "No one has asked me how I feel," she said.

She began crying and said, "I feel silly crying. I don't want to be a burden." 100% of her believed that crying in front of me was burdensome. I began tapping the karate chop point on these general thoughts and feelings.

SETUP:

Even though I feel silly crying about this accident, I deeply and completely love and accept myself.

Even though no one has asked me how I feel until now, I know that God cares about how I feel, and loves me equally when I am upset and when I am not.

Even though I feel like a burden crying, I love and forgive myself for crying about this major accident.

We tapped on the reminder statements of: "This accident, No one seems to care, A part of me feels silly, I feel like a burden, No one thinks to ask how I am."

I told Kristina to change my words if they did not resonate with her. If my words did not connect with her truth, she could replace them at any time.

We tapped through the body and face points three times. When her tears stopped, and her shoulders relaxed, I asked her how she was feeling.

There was a complete shift in her attitude. She thought it was ridiculous that she shouldn't cry, when she could have been killed. Crying was a normal response! She recognized that when people didn't ask her about the event, it wasn't because they didn't care. They just didn't know what to say. It was the awkwardness, or lack of understanding, that made them not ask. When I asked for her SUDS level on feeling like a burden, she said it sounded ridiculous, and gave it a 0.

I asked her if she felt ready to talk about the actual event. She was ready.

When she recalled the day, she felt afraid that God lost trust in her. She could feel the fear in her heart at a SUDS level of 8. I told her to explain further, and she began telling me the story.

"I was walking along the road, and," she paused, "I should have known better. I didn't use the crosswalk. I remember thinking I should, and then I didn't. I am afraid that God lost trust in me. I couldn't even listen to my intuition in that moment. Why would He trust me with bigger things?"

SETUP:

Even though I didn't use the crosswalk, I love myself and forgive myself for my choices, past and present.

Even though I knew to use the crosswalk and didn't, I accept Jesus' forgiveness and love in my strengths and my weaknesses.

Even though I heard my intuition and didn't trust it, and I might not be trusted with bigger things, I forgive myself and embrace Jesus' forgiveness and grace.

Even though I fear that God won't trust me with bigger things, I am open to His forgiveness and trust now and in the future.

REMINDERS:

I didn't trust my intuition and now I think God can't trust me
He might never trust me now that I made one mistake
I saw the crosswalk and chose not to use it

I could have avoided this
I knew better than to cross the street
I should have known better
I feel so afraid because of that moment

God might never trust me now
God might punish me

I did another two rounds of tapping. I noticed that she no longer agreed with the statement, "He doesn't trust me." I asked about the SUDS level, and she said it had dropped to a 4.

"I hate making mistakes. If I had listened to my gut, I wouldn't have messed up."

Her SUDS level on making mistakes was a 10. We began tapping the face and body points.

I hate making mistakes and this was a big mistake
If only I had listened to my gut. The Holy Spirit was talking
I wouldn't have been hit
I could have avoided this pain if only I had listened
God might not trust me now because I messed up
Because I made such a big mistake, He won't forgive me for a thing like this
This mistake is too big for Jesus
Even Jesus' forgiveness won't cover this

I use exaggeration to spur reframes from the client. I asked her what she was thinking and feeling. She recalled how she actually became closer to God and other people through this experience. With her rational mind engaged, she was seeing that she was already forgiven. She even recalled that she had just been asked to speak on a volunteer trip with her church, a symbol of God's trust.

The SUDS level regarding making mistakes dropped to a 1 from a 10, and regarding God's lack of trust dropped from a 4 to a 0.

[*Sherrie's comment:* Notice the flow of the session. The SUDS dropped on one aspect (detail) of the memory and immediately another aspect reared its head just like another mountain range on the prairie horizon that Kristina must cross to clear out as much emotional content as possible from this memory.]

She continued with her story from a neutral point. She didn't remember being hit, but recalled the moments after the car hit her: "I didn't feel anything at first when I became conscious, then I felt my legs hurt. I knew I was on the pavement, but I was so scared to open my eyes. I didn't know if my legs were broken. I didn't know if I had brain damage. I didn't want to be paralyzed. I was so afraid of what I would see if I looked."

Her SUDS level on her fear of opening her eyes was a 10.

I was too afraid to open my eyes
I was on the pavement and couldn't feel anything
I was so scared; what if I had brain damage?
What if I would never be the same?
I didn't want to look or find out what had happened
I was afraid my legs were broken
I was afraid I was paralyzed and I wouldn't be of any help to Jesus again
I was afraid that I had brain damage
I was thinking the worst; my legs hurt so badly
I thought I might be paralyzed
I was so scared
I was afraid to find out the truth!

We tapped for three rounds and I added, "Even though I thought I would have brain damage, I don't! Even though I was scared that I would be paralyzed, I was wrong! The truth is..."

I asked her to share her thoughts now that she knew the outcome of the accident. She felt so relieved. She had carried all that fear of "what will happen," even though she knew the ending to the story... a much happier ending than she had imagined.

I checked in on the SUDS level for "fear of opening her eyes." It was down to a 0.

I asked her to continue with her story while tapping the karate chop point, beginning at a neutral place in the story. She now recalled a few detailed aspects that she had blocked out. "I actually saw the car rounding the corner. I was in the middle of the street. I couldn't do anything about it. I just had to brace myself for what happened next."

I asked her for the emotion on seeing the car. She said she felt helpless with a SUDS level of 10.

We began tapping the face and body points. I interjected questions as we tapped.

I was so helpless, the car was rounding the corner
I was in the middle of the street
It was moving too fast
I felt so helpless, there was nothing I could do except brace myself
I braced myself for the worst and it was all out of my control

After 2 rounds her shoulders relaxed, and reported that the SUDS level on seeing the car was a 4. I asked her to describe the car for me and tap the face points, as she talked.

[**Sherrie's comment:** It often is these detailed sensory points that pin the memory in place, just like the earlier story of the green pick-up truck.]

It was a blue car, fast looking

A male driver
Speedy looking sedan
It came out of nowhere
There was nothing I could do
It was all slow motion
But so fast so helpless

The SUDS regarding the image of the car dropped to a 0. I asked her, "What were you thinking when you saw the car?"

"Who will take care of my family?" she said. She felt extreme sadness for her family, as if they were helpless without her. Her sadness and fear for them was at a 9, in her chest.

I used the karate chop point.

SET-UP:

Even though I worried about who would take care of my family, I trust that God takes care of them even when I cannot.

When I knew I was about to be hit, my first thought was about my family, and I honor and respect myself for why I carry that fear.

Even though I worry about my family, even when I am the one in danger, I trust that God cares for them and myself, and I forgive myself for all the moments I cannot care for them.

Even though I feel helpless and sad for my family, I deeply love and accept them and myself.

REMINDER PHRASES:

I was about to be hit and I worried about my family
I was so afraid
Who will take care of my family?
It is my job to take care of them
If I can't, no one else will
I feel so helpless for them
I feel so sad at the thought of this
If something happens to me, no one else will be there for them
They need me to be here
If I get hurt, they will be so unsafe
This is my job
It's my job, and NO ONE else's to protect them
This feeling in my heart
Reminds me to protect them
I love them so much
I worry about who will care for them

Sometimes, I use exaggeration to reveal to clients moments when we have taken a role that God wants to take back from us. In this case, the exaggeration helped. She saw that God is the main caretaker, and that she is just a vessel.

God worked through her for years to help her family, who struggled emotionally and spiritually. Even when she was gone, God would continue to support them. We made a note that she could pray and tap on early moments when she felt like she had to take the role of caretaker.

She still had tears in her eyes, but now it was because she felt her heart opening with compassion. The feeling in her heart had changed from sadness to *love for her family. She honored that God made her to put others above her-self, but that she was never meant to do it alone.*

I prompted her to begin the story again from a neutral point. This time, when she recalled coming to consciousness, she remembers praying to God that she would be okay. "My legs hurt and I started praying, but stopped. For some reason I thought God couldn't hear my prayers. I felt like he wasn't listening to me. I don't know why. I felt like I had made such a mistake." She said that she felt sadness at a SUDS level of 7.

We tapped three rounds on the face and body points as I said her words in various ways:

I felt so sad
I still feel sad
I stopped praying
Because God wasn't listening
That is what it felt like at the time
I had made such a mistake
I felt like God wouldn't listen to my prayers
Not anymore
Not after such a huge mistake
He couldn't hear my prayers
He didn't hear my prayer
He chose not to hear my prayer
That's what I thought in that moment
Because I had made a mistake
And I thought God would forgive my mistake
So I stopped praying
My legs hurt
And I immediately prayed
But I stopped
Because I thought God wouldn't listen
When we make mistakes

Her eyes brightened. "He was listening! My screams brought people out of the stores. There was a man who came over and immediately started helping me. He began telling me everything was okay. I opened my eyes and saw blood on the pavement, but he said I was okay."

I asked her about her screams bringing people out of the store. She said her SUDS was a 5 on the scream and a 7 on the blood. Her SUDS for the sadness about stopping the prayer was now a 3.

I asked her to explain more about the man as we tapped:

My screams brought people out of the store
It must of hurt a lot
I don't remember screaming
The man told me
My scream was that loud
When I opened my eyes, he was there
He was being so nice
I don't know where he came from
I saw blood on the pavement
I was so scared
I didn't know my leg was broken
He said I was fine
But I was terrified
I felt like it was a dream
I don't know where the man came from
But he was my answered prayer
He told me it would all be okay
He was right!

We stopped to take a breather and check-in. She was crying with joy now as she recalled the event. Her SUDS level about her unheard prayer was a 0 instead of a 3. She said that this man was her answered prayer. She felt like God sent an angel to her through this man. When she thought of the blood, it felt more distant, like it was a memory instead of right in front of her face. She told me that God must have been involved because the doctors said her cast would be on for a few months and it only took one!

The SUDS levels on the image of blood and the sound of her own screaming was also a 0.

We went back through the story while tapping the Karate Chop point, and she recalled all of it without any emotional peaks.

We ended by sneaking away[74] on her initial fears. She still feared, at a 4 intensity, that she might experience the symptoms again. I incorporated a few positive reframes that came up in our debrief discussion.

I am still afraid of having future fears
I am afraid of future stress symptoms
But God healed my leg in record time
And he might heal these symptoms
People might not care to talk about the accident
But that won't stop me from talking about healing
I was afraid God didn't trust me
But He trusts me in my weakness and my strength
I was afraid He wasn't listening
But He sent a man to help
He sent His healing
I felt like a burden talking about this
But God loves to listen
God loves to heal
God loves to use this for His good
And a lot of good came from this
I learned that God was with me
That He forgives me
That He listens to me
And that He heals
Even when I doubt
Even when I am afraid
Even when I am helpless
I am thankful for His forgiveness
And for His care
And for His unconditional love
I am open to listening to my intuition
And trusting God
To use this moment for the good of others
More and more every day!

---

74   "Sneaking away" is an EFT technique that we use at the end of a session when appointment time runs out if any intensity is left in the issue that is being worked on.

I asked her how she felt. She was about to leave on a volunteer trip to speak at a women's leadership conference in Bangladesh. She looked back at the post-traumatic symptoms and accident as a way to inspire the women she would speak with in just a few weeks. She said that she knows God will use this story for His purposes on her upcoming trip.

This session was so revealing about the character of God for both the client and me. For one, He uses all circumstances for good in the end (Romans 8:28). Secondly, He answers prayers through other people, even when we doubt. Third, He covers all fears, all shame and all weakness in His forgiveness. We just need to remove our fear and shame in order to see it!

I checked in with her the following week for a follow-up session. She hadn't experienced any of the symptoms or thoughts she reported initially, and the self-forgiveness she achieved in the initial session still resonated long and clear with her. She chose to address a different childhood topic in the follow-up based on a few core beliefs that arose in the accident. She recalls the accident as a symbol that God is the ultimate caretaker, and healer.

BIO:
Jackie Viramontez is a Certified EFT Practitioner and Life Coach in Los Angeles, CA. She is committed to helping Christian and secular clients find freedom from the beliefs, fears and idols that hold them captive.

She believes that fear and trauma are opportunities for healing and growth. Her experiences with childhood trauma and sexual abuse have made her an advocate for women who have the right to feel safe, loved and beautiful. She guides women back to their true identity, power and freedom with EFT Tapping and strengths-based coaching.[75]

EFT AS OUR GPS BY CHARITY KAYEMBE

If forgiveness is our destination, then EFT is the roadmap to get us there. We all know we should walk in forgiveness. We are aware the Bible instructs us to do this and we understand how harboring bitterness and unforgiveness is like drinking poison and expecting the other person to be harmed. If for no other reason than enlightened self-interest, we know we must forgive!

---

75 Find out more at www.jackieviramontez.com

But knowing we should and the actually doing can feel like a world apart and even though we want to get there, we just don't know how. The good we want to do we're not doing, as the inner warzone of Romans 7 is played out time and again in our hearts and minds. How do we make this work?

Enter tapping. It makes the biblical truths we want to walk in more available, accessible, and doable. I will share a personal example to illustrate my impassioned struggle with forgiveness and how the gift of EFT was the only process that helped.

I had experienced a deep violation of trust, and in my mind, betrayal. I was devastated and couldn't stop thinking about what had happened, replaying conversations again and again, trying to make sense of the pain. Had I done something wrong? I was hurt, angry and confused.

Of course, I know the verses. I am fully aware I need to love and forgive. However, that kind of emotional freedom was on the other side of the great chasm of despair in which I currently found myself. And I couldn't get to the other side on my own.

I prayed; I cried out to God. I confessed, repented, and quoted Scripture. I even practiced EFT. But it didn't take, so I called Sherrie.

Sherrie teaches that for everyday things, after you have dealt with the greater baggage from your past, you can do well tapping for yourself. But when major drama and trauma comes up, it really helps to tap with someone with more experience in the heavier issues of life. That is why I called.

Over the course of two weeks, Sherrie tapped with me three different times over the phone. We talked and tapped for about an hour each time. I always cried, and she always prayed. And, we always tapped negative. There was nothing good I could see in the situation, nothing positive that I could focus on. So we tapped and tapped until every drop of anger, resentment, confusion and sadness were gone. I was literally tapped out.

After three sessions of nothing but negatives, I had finally cleared enough space in my heart for some positives to have room to live and grow. It was in this place on my journey of healing that God gave me a dream, and the message from that dream held the truths He wanted me to now tap down into my heart and into my very cells.

TAPPING IN TRUTH

My dream included two main scenes. In the first, I was on a movie set. I was an extra in the film, and the camera quickly panned over the crowd. I was in the shot for the briefest of moments. That was my entire part in the movie. If you blinked, you would have missed me!

In the second scene, I was riding atop the shell of a giant tortoise on the lake next to the film crew. With me on its back, the tortoise dove deep underwater and went all the way down to the bottom of the lake. It was a fun ride, and it felt good down there!

This was a dream picture of Second Corinthians 4, and Holy Spirit especially highlighted for me the last few verses of that chapter:

> *"Therefore we do not lose heart. Though outwardly we are wasting away, yet inwardly we are being renewed day by day. For our light and momentary troubles are achieving for us an eternal glory that far outweighs them all. So we fix our eyes not on what is seen, but on what is unseen, since what is seen is temporary, but what is unseen is eternal."* (2 Corinthians 4:16–18)

Through the dream symbols, God was saying, "Don't lose heart, be renewed in Me. The trouble you're going through is light and momentary, just like your scene in the movie. It was so quick, and then it was over! This too shall pass."

God explained the play on words in my dream: "Charity, don't look at that movie *scene*, that is, don't look at what is *seen*. Don't focus on that painful event because that was only temporary. Look at what is unseen because that is what lasts and is eternal."

In the dream, what was unseen was the bottom of the lake. It was deep and hidden, and I had to ride down to it on the tortoise's back. Animals often represent emotions in our dreams, and to me, a tortoise is "eternal." They live hundreds of years, longer than any other animal, so this symbol was the ideal of eternity to me.

Whose emotions are eternal? Holy Spirit's, of course. Love, joy and peace are godly emotions that last forever. They are outside of time and not dependent on this temporary world and the circumstances in it. They are the emotions of Heaven. But how can I connect with them?

Holy Spirit also revealed that secret through the dream. He explained, "You just have to do in waking life what you did in the dream. You went down deep. You didn't stay on the surface, with superficial, environmentally dependent emotions. You went down under, into the unseen depths of your spirit. It's in your inner man that My Spirit joins your spirit. It is down deep inside your heart where you can always find Me and My presence and My peace and My joy.

"The pain is a temporary movie scene. Don't look at the pain that is seen in the natural. Go down deep into your spirit and connect with My heart within yours. There you will find peace that can't be explained and joy that can't be taken away. Fix your eyes on Me and live into My kingdom within. That's what is eternal. Eternity is in your heart."

Praise God for His perspective, His instruction, and His grace to obey! So now that I have received this night vision from Heaven and accompanying *rhema* (spoken word) revelation from the Lord, what do I do with it?

I tap it in. I ponder it and remember it. And when I'm tempted to look at the painful situation in waking life, I go back to the picture God gave me through my dream. And I tap. That is my new truth. I'm being renewed day by day in my inner man. I'm living from the mind of Christ and His view of my situation. I'm being transformed into His image as I look where He directs my focus. I meditate and I tap it in. I picture Jesus with me and I tap that in. I ponder His truth, His perception, His wisdom and His understanding, and I tap it all in. It is a supernatural exchange of my ashes for His beauty and my tears for His joy. And I am changed.

[**Sherrie's comment:** We almost always need to tap negatively, but this is one of the exceptions. Once Charity tapped until the negative emotions were a zero SUDS, she could then "tap in"—through prayer or meditation—God's Truth.]

TRUE FEELING

We know the right Scriptures; the problem is we don't always feel them. They don't feel true to us. Does that matter? Yes, it most certainly does. When I first got into tapping, I often heard the then curious phrase: "Does that feel true to you?"

Huh? What in the world kind of question is that, anyway?

"God loves you, and He's forgiven your sin. Does that feel true to you?"

Are you kidding? I don't care how it feels. That *is* true. That is Scriptural truth! You can't argue with that, for goodness sake. "God said it. I believe it. That settles it!"

Well, that's all well and good, but believing it in my head doesn't make it true in my heart because God's love is not experienced in my head; love is experienced in my heart. Christ's forgiveness is not felt in my head; it's felt in my heart. These are spirit-level realities, and God wants us to feel they are true for us personally. He wants us to experience these biblical truths with heart understanding (Isaiah 6:10).

[**Sherrie's comment:** I had an old pastor who once repeatedly said this, "The longest 18 inches in history is between a Christian's head and his heart."]

In my book *Hearing God Through Your Dreams*[76], I teach that dreams are a form of meditation that move scriptural truth from our heads to our hearts. Tapping does the same thing. Tapping makes the promises of the Bible personal and revelational.

Whether we believe the Bible or not, it is still true. But God doesn't just want His truth memorized in our brains; He wants His truth written on our hearts. Then it is no longer just biblical truth, it is our truth, too. We own it. God wants His Word made flesh in us, and He can use tapping to do it.

---

76   Virkler and Kayembe, *Hearing God Through Your Dreams*, 2016.

SUB-SECTION THREE:
Tapping <u>Away</u> Negative Emotions

CHAPTER 13

Worry and Anxiety

Worry is a sinful habit. Friends and family often tell us, "I'm just a worry wart!" They wear that title like a badge of honor or courage, as if they are doing all of us for whom they worry a great big favor.

Sometimes, people take this worrying one step too far! If no one is sick, no financial calamity looms, or no recent accidents or international incidents happen, then they worry about having nothing to worry about! I remember my grandma using the term "worry" in an interesting way. She'd say, "Stop worrying that shirt sleeve, you will wear it out." Worry does wear us out!

According to Dictionary.com, the definition of *worry* includes:

To torment oneself with or suffer from disturbing thoughts; fret.
To torment with cares, anxieties, etc.; trouble; plague.
To seize, especially by the throat, with the teeth and shake or mangle, as one animal does to another.

The entry that catches my eye is the latter one. At times, we literally grab our worry by the throat, bury our teeth in it, and hang on like we'll lose something precious if we let it go. It reminds me of a toddler hanging onto a toy for dear life. No friend or foe is going to rip that toy out of that child's hands; they defend it with every fiber of their being.

Why do we do this? Worry affects 40 million people in this country. I don't mean short-lived day-to-day concerns like a crying child, a rattling muffler, an unexpected bill in the mail, or a phone call in the middle of the night.

The worry that keeps millions of Americans awake at night is chronic. We go from one worry right into the next, or pile the worries up like cordwood awaiting a cold Maine winter. We seem to never have enough worries to worry about, even though worry wears us out emotionally, spiritually, and physically.

The Bible abounds with multiple verses regarding worry. Jesus knew worry was a plague on society. Matthew 6:25–27, Philippians 4:6, Hebrews 13:5–6, Matthew 11:28–30, Luke 12:22–31, Psalm 55:22, Isaiah 41:10, John 14:1 are among several of the verses in Scripture that clearly tell us to leave all things in the hands of our Lord.

In a Matthew Poole commentary, he presents a different twist on worry from Matthew 6:33:

> "The kingdom of God, and his righteousness, in this verse, are terms comprehensive of whatsoever appertaineth to the honour and glory of God, either as means, or as the end. Let your principal care and study be how to get to heaven, and how to promote the kingdom of God in the world; to bring your hearts into subjection to the will of God, that the kingdom of God may be within you, and how to bring others to the obedience of faith and of the will of God. And for the things of this life, it shall fare with you as it did with Solomon, 1 Kings 3:12, who asked not riches and honour, but had them. You shall have for your necessities, Psalm 37:4, Mark 10:30, 1 Timothy 4:8."[77]

We often put our human focus on the wrong things, and much of the time we know it. As Christians, we understand that in the end, what we see or experience here on earth has little to do with our eternity in heaven with our Savior. Although we are responsible for living an upright, Godly life, we know Jesus Christ died at Calvary on the cross for our sins, giving us a heavenly future. On that sacrifice is what we should maintain our focus, not fretting day to day about earthly affairs, particularly ones we cannot control; we can do nothing to fix them.

But we also know we *must get* through this life first. Much of life is like a chore that many of us wish to forego for the greater glory awaiting us. God sees it differently because each of us has a divinely ordained purpose in this life here on earth.

So, how do we turn all this worry and concern for our present life over to God?

---

77 Poole, Matthew, "Commentary on 6:33." Matthew Poole's English Annotations on the Holy Bible. www.studylight.org/commentaries/mpc/matthew-6.html

That's a great question, and one that I personally struggled with for decades. The harder I tried to leave it all in God's hands, the more I worried. Then I worried I couldn't leave it in God's hands, compounding the problem even more. That left me worrying that I didn't have enough faith in God. I struggled and worked harder to secure more faith only to fail again, causing more worry. It all felt like a never-ending cycle of work, doubt, and worry.

I struggled to get to the place where I could heed the advice of Matthew 6:33— Seeking God's Kingdom first, allowing Him to take care of all of life's details, knowing we are safely nestled in His loving arms. Instead, I worried and I ruminated.

The word "worry" concentrates primarily on future events that may happen; whereas, the word "ruminate" emphasizes concerns for past events or memories. Both types have a basis in perception, and both words are based in worry. We perceive or interpret what happened in the past or we anticipate what may or might happen in the future, based on our experiences of the past. If it took you 8 months to find a new job the last time you were laid off from work, you will worry it may take at least that long, if not longer, the next time you need to find new employment. Worry is based on perceptions built around past experiences.

Ruminating about the past includes *what ifs. What if I had done something differently? Would my life and present day circumstances be any different?* Similarly, heavily over-thinking how poorly treated you were by people around you leads you deeper into perceptions and conclusions that may or may not be true. Many of these perceptions are personal in nature.

In both cases of worry, it's your own personal thought processes that perceive how something did or did not work out previously for you, or something that may or may not work out for you in the future. But God's Word clearly tells us, "Do not be anxious about anything, but in every situation, by prayer and petition, with thanksgiving, present your requests to God" (Philippians 4:6).

Dr. Robert Leahy explains that worry and stress can get us into physical trouble.[78] Although I don't necessarily agree with the author's conclusion of how to stop worrying because I advocate tapping instead, the article does offer great insights.

---

78 www.huffingtonpost.com/robert-leahy-phd/dwelling-on-the-negative-_b_799103.html

I was taught that for every hour of thinking about a subject or thought, the synaptic neural connections around that idea double.[79] Therefore, all worry and ruminating digs us into a deeper sinkhole emotionally.

WHAT WORRY DOES TO OUR BRAIN

Worry has deep neurophysiological roots, based in anxiety and it can lead to panic attacks and obsessive-compulsive type behavior, eventually trending toward possible post-traumatic disorder symptoms.

> "Emotional experiences become imprinted in your brain cells and memory and form patterns that influence your behavior. Strong negative emotional states are more likely to be remembered than positive ones."[80]

Because we develop worry and anxiety over time, the brain progressively learns how to be anxious, memory by memory, and event by event. The associations of those memories and events begin to cognitively structure your mind, teaching you step by step how to think and behave. It becomes a pattern, a habit, and a trap. The mind learns how and what to be afraid of. If you're afraid of a certain event or memory, and this triggers your anxiety or fear, the neurons in your brain fire together, and over time, they wire together around that exact anxiety or fear.[81]

> "Memories are made in individual cells. It consists of an association between a group of neurons such that when one fires, they all fire, creating a specific pattern."[82] This is based on the research of Donald Hebbs.[83]

God created our brain structure to recognize fear. The amygdala makes the recognition and sends the message on to the hippocampus to decide if any situations you have encountered in the past have similarities to this new situation, and if so, asks if it is dangerous.

With each experience, your neurology creates new neural pathways or grows already existing ones—very similar to the continental railroad system—carrying information from one neuron to the next. The neurons cling together in bundles and associate with one another as one thought leads you to think of another, or as one memory must be understood in order to make sense of future ones. The feel-

---

79 Church, *The Genie in Your Genes*, 100.
80 Childre, *The HeartMath Solution*, 137–138, 203.
81 Church, *The Genie in Your Genes*, 105.
82 Carter, ed., *Mapping the Mind*, 159.
83 Dispenza, *Evolve Your Brain*, 184–185.

ing of anxiety is often a rush of adrenaline and cortisol, two of the most prevalent hormones in our body.

As you learn—whether educational facts, emotional tendencies, or other information—you wire together billions of neural cells into vast cognitive associations. Worry takes over when negative emotional issues surface. It is hardwired into the mind with those neurochemicals, a mix that is uniquely your own, and then the neurochemicals cement it all together.[84]

Every time a memory or event triggers your mind, it brings you back to the part of the event that was most unpleasant or the part that didn't work out so well for you, and your neurochemistry once again releases a mixture of adrenaline and cortisol (and other neurochemicals) that makes your heart race, your blood pressure rise, and your blood sugar elevate, clouding your thinking process around what is happening in the present.[85]

When you are stressed, 70–80% of the blood in your neocortex, the thinking part of your brain, rushes to your larger arm and leg muscles because your mind thinks you must fight or run from the stressor. This fight or flight reaction happens even if there is no real danger because the mind also sees worry as a real threat.

TEST ANXIETY

Children who routinely do poorly on exams also have this same mechanism running in their neocortex. Once they *fear* exams, their bodies will put them into full flight or fight just thinking about a test. The child really cannot answer the exam questions because 70–80% of the blood needed to think has drained out of their neocortex into their larger fighting muscles all because the mind thinks the test is dangerous!

I teach children with test anxiety to tap just before the teacher hands out the test. It usually only takes less than a minute of tapping to calm the amygdala (fear center in the brain) down so it allows the blood to return to the neocortex so the child can process the test questions well.[86]

With every trigger—real or perceived, including failed tests, whether it is conscious or subconscious—you reinforce the worry and fear deeper and stronger

---

84   Ibid., 100–101.
85   Church, *The Genie in Your Genes*, 171.
86   Ibid., 172.

into your neural connections. You trap yourself. You find yourself stuck in a process you know is harming you, but it feels completely out of control. You ask God to take away the worry, but it often seems He is not listening. This could be viewed as a spiritual problem underpinned with a physical neurological issue.

GIFTS OF HEALINGS

God heals in different ways, through many different gifts of healings (1 Corinthians 12:9). Sometimes when we pray asking for deliverance from a problem, God heals us instantaneously with a supernatural miracle. That is certainly our preference! However, many times God uses His created mechanisms to allow us to heal. Doctors, medicine, herbs, tonics, deliverance, fasting, dietary changes, to name a few, are great examples of this type of healing. But there is another – Emotional Freedom Techniques.

During the actual act of tapping, we change those specific neural pathways that keep us stuck in the behavior we so loathe—the behaviors that we know are keeping us from allowing God to care for us, worry-free, to permit us to move out into the world to enjoy the beauty and relationships He has bestowed on us.

As we tap negatively, the subconscious mind recognizes and knows where those worry connections live within our bodies, and it begins to sever them. The beauty of this process is often tapping removes large bundles of negative connections within a very short period of time. It's like a great big computer. The mind knows where it has stored every event or memory you have ever experienced. It knows where to go to find the problem. In EFT we call this the "generalization effect." This is similar to someone knocking down a transformer and taking out an entire neighborhood's power grid along with it.

UNLEARNING WORRY

There is a specific EFT process that needs to be done; just tapping anywhere in any old manner probably won't solve the anxiety issue. As we tap, we must go back and allow our bodies to feel the worry and anxiety, asking the Holy Spirit to bring to our mind specifically what memories in our past match the present-day feeling, or what does the feeling remind us of.

Those are the memories that underscore where and how this bad habit of worry started, and where the neurochemical mix has its basis. Worry is a learned habit—much like reciting your ABCs is a learned skill.

By tapping out the emotions felt today about memories of long-past days, God will often break that long-standing habit of worry and anxiety, freeing you to trust Him implicitly for your every need.

Brenda Cordle is a performance coach, speaker, and writer who helps athletes and performing artists understand how to raise performance ceilings and lower performance anxiety so her clients can "nail it," even when the pressure is on. Understanding the critical role emotional wellness plays in achieving one's goals, she's also a Certified EFT Coach[87], and teaches her clients to use this tool to improve their skills and optimize their performance. To illustrate EFT's effectiveness with worry and anxiety, Brenda shares the following story.

EMMA'S STORY—A TEEN'S DEBILITATING ANXIETY

A ninth grader I'll call Emma was referred to me by her school's guidance counselor. She had been suffering from severe anxiety and resisted going to school every day. She refused to eat lunch in the lunchroom because it made her extremely anxious. For months she had been eating lunch in a classroom with a teacher who had volunteered to eat with her because of her situation. The anxiety had been a problem for Emma for about two years. She had been treated by a physician for anxiety and depression previously and was still dealing with earlier issues when I received the phone call from her mother.

I included Emma's mom in the first session, as I typically do with youngsters. Neither of them were familiar with EFT, and I especially wanted mom to understand how EFT works so she could be supportive of Emma and help her use the tool at home. From the intake forms and first session interview, I learned more about her situation, including the following: 1.) The anxiety started while the family was living abroad due to her father's employment. The family moved back to the States earlier than planned because of Emma's struggle with anxiety and depression. 2.) A close family member had been killed on active duty in Afghanistan when Emma was 12 years old. It was a very challenging time for the family, and it had a big impact on Emma. 3.) At age 10, she had been bullied by a few older girls at the dance studio where she took dance lessons and competed on a dance team. She had been through counseling as a result of this. However, even after counseling, Emma clung to her mom and would not leave her side for quite some time. 4.) At age four, Emma got into an elevator and the doors closed very quickly before her mom

87 www.BrendaCordle.com

could get in. She was separated from her Mom for 10 – 15 minutes while her mother tried to find out where she was. After that incident, she started stuttering and did so for several years. She refused to get on elevators until she was 12, and she was still very scared of them. 5.) An HST Assessment revealed that she registered very high on the scale of "Highly Sensitive Temperament."

With plenty of material to work on, I started by teaching both Emma and her Mom the EFT basic process. I instructed them how to use EFT as "first aid" when she felt herself getting anxious. In the first session, we began tapping about the lunchroom. I asked her to pretend my office door led to the lunchroom and asked her, on a scale of 0–10, how afraid are you to enter that room? It was a 10. I took the following approach:

SETUP:

Even though I'm afraid to go in that lunchroom, I know God loves me completely, and I know I'm going to be okay.

Even though I'm afraid to go in that lunchroom, I accept myself just the way I am anyway.

Even though I'm afraid to go in that lunchroom, I know God loves me and I accept myself just the way I am, even when I'm afraid.

Then I asked her to follow me in tapping through the acupressure points while telling me the reasons she was afraid to go into the lunchroom. These included: it's very loud, there are lots of older kids in there, people make fun of other people, there are so many people in there, I get angry when I go in there, kids are mean to me.

After the first round, her SUD number was 9, and I had lots of tapping material! For the next several rounds, I used her words and tapped though each of the things she told me about the lunchroom. It's too loud, people make fun of others, there are so many people, etc. Her numbers decreased gradually through several rounds. She was down to a 3 when the session was over. I gave her a homework assignment to become more aware of the thoughts she was having about why she did not want to go school, and tap at least a few rounds each morning during her drive there with her mom.

[*Sherrie's comment:* You will notice that Brenda started with a present day problem first before venturing back in time to tackle Emma's earlier issues. This is a gentler way of applying EFT, giving the client a chance to experience the effects of how EFT feels and it allows God to possibly dismantle other related issues by the "generalization effect."]

I met with Emma alone when she returned for her second session. I learned she had been having some better days as well as some very anxious days since I saw her last. She was still eating lunch in a classroom every day as a result. Without her mom present, she was much more willing to talk to me about specific details. I started the session by asking her to walk me through her typical school day, tell me about each class, what she liked, what she did not like, and what made her anxious.

[*Sherrie's comment:* When we first begin tapping with clients, this often is their experience. They "pendulate", a word coined by Dr. Peter Levine, between feeling relief and triggering as the body-mind attempts to re-adjust to a new safer, thought process.[88]]

I quickly learned she was very sad about a relationship with a particular friend she had met at the beginning of the school year. Emma was the "new girl" at the beginning of the year, and she was excited to make a good friend quickly. However, after a few months, the friendship went awry. The new friend stopped hanging out with her without much of an explanation. Emma had a few other friends, but felt betrayed by the new friend who had began the school year spending a lot of time with her and giving her a lot of attention. After the friendship cooled, Emma withdrew and became very anxious in response. She stopped going to the lunchroom because this friend sat at "her" lunch table, and Emma was very uncomfortable being there now.

While tapping with me, she was able to express her anger, embarrassment, and other emotions she was having about the new school and the broken friendship. As her SUD number decreased with more tapping rounds, she began to gain more perspective on the other friendships she still maintained, and realized there were many students and teachers in the school who sincerely cared about her.

---

88 Levine, *In An Unspoken Voice*, 55–56.

At Emma's third session, I was startled to see her looking completely different! She was standing taller and had a spring in her step. She smiled and seemed at ease. I learned she had been back in the lunchroom every day and sitting at the same table with the friend who had hurt her so deeply. So during this session, we focused on the bullying she had experienced at the dance studio at age 10. We tapped through the details of becoming a competitive dancer at that young age, how much pressure she put on herself to be perfect, and how devastated she was when a few older dancers treated her badly.

[**Sherrie's comment:** Clients lead us to what they want to tap on next.]

Their comments about her body and their disapproval of her dance skills were very hurtful at the time. For a child with an HST personality, this type of treatment can be very challenging to overcome. As a result, she felt she could never be good enough to fit in, and these feelings of inadequacy made her feel very unsafe. This spilled over into other situations at school and her church youth group over the next few years. She felt as if no one liked her and always felt uncomfortable in social situations. The entire session was spent tapping on these issues, and she began to feel much better about it. Her SUD was 9 when we began, and ended at 1.

When I asked Emma for an update at her fourth session, she referred to the broken friendship discussed earlier and said, "It doesn't faze me anymore." She told me she was still sitting at the same table, and that she had been having some conversations with the friend during lunch lately. She reported her anxiety was much lower overall with just an occasional spike. We then spent the remainder of the session talking about the family member who had been killed in Afghanistan and processing some of her deep grief over that loss.

Emma's fifth and last session was exactly one month after her first session. She seemed completely at ease with all the issues we had discussed in earlier sessions. She told me these were all behind her now and she was "moving on with my life." The only outstanding issue from her history of past hurts was the fear of elevators. There is an elevator in my office building, so we spent the session getting over that fear. First, we stood outside the elevator and tapped for a few minutes. Then we pushed the button, got into the elevator, and tapped while riding it up and down several times. She told me she was no longer afraid of elevators at the conclusion of our session.

While I have not seen Emma since, I was informed by the school's counselor she is doing well.

You see, you, like Emma, learned the bad habit that plagues you somewhere, most likely in early childhood or young adulthood. If you go back to an earlier event, recalling all the intricate details of whatever the memory was, dismantling it piece by sensory piece, all the while tapping, you can often solve your problem—and often permanently. Sometimes, the memory is so traumatic that the subconscious mind refuses to remember it. In such cases, a seasoned Christian EFT practitioner can tap with you using one of the several "Gentle Techniques" that can neutralize the emotions around a memory in a more roundabout way.

MY BATTLE WITH WORRY

I was probably the world's best worrier! I would lay awake nights on end with my stomach in knots, sweating profusely, mind ruminating over and over about events long past, knowing I could do absolutely nothing to change what I did or what was done to me. The event was over. Worrying wasn't going to change a thing, so why continue to worry? Do-overs are not an available option.

Such thoughts often lead to self-commentary on what I thought about myself, "Boy, am I stupid for doing that," or "No one loves me or she wouldn't have done that to me," or "It's all my fault that didn't work out the way I thought it would." Each of us has many self-deprecating thoughts, and each comes out of worry over something we couldn't control, or we didn't control to our liking. It is most often about our self-centered idea that we are in control of our destiny. Worry doubts the sovereignty of God. It is walking in disobedience because we are told to trust God with our whole heart regarding every aspect of our lives.

And in my heart I understood this theological concept, and it made me even more upset that I could not let go and allow God to handle both my past and future right here and now in the present.

With repetition, we instill into ourselves and carry those thoughts forward in our lives, replicating again and again the same behavior we hate, making it our reality—a life based on faulty worry perceptions of years past. We are often our own worst enemy, making the exact thing we fear come true in our lives. Job did this (Job 3:25). We ought not follow his example!

Tapping can often eliminate these thought processes permanently. As we tap away the negatives of the past, the future becomes fully alive. Fears and uncertainty about the future fade away. God has it all under control; we have no need to concern ourselves about it. We can then live in the moment, knowing we are held securely in His arms, totally safe in His love.

It is in that day-to-day mindfulness that our bodies heal. Our cortisol level drops to acceptable levels and our immune system recovers.

God was faithful in my life, and He did all of that for me, and He can do it for you. What amazes me now is when I find myself awake at night, the thoughts rarely dwell on the past, but instead they dwell on the future and what I can do for God to move His Kingdom forward for the benefit of mankind. I lay in bed praying, tapping and asking God for His guidance to tell me exactly what it is He wants me to do for Him. It's amazing!

Through EFT, God has put to bed my rumination of already done past events and memories. God came into my life with His industrial broom and simply swept my emotional baggage back into the past where it belongs.

And He's waiting to do it for you, too! Our loving heavenly Father always takes care of the little details better than we ever could, blessing us "immeasurably more than all we ask or imagine, according to his power that is at work within us" (Ephesians 3:20). EFT can be an extremely effective way to tap into that power.

CHAPTER 14

Bad Habits

In Emotional Freedom Techniques, we teach, "nothing is as it appears to be." What does that mean? Most habits— bad, good or otherwise—have an under-pinning to something we learned as a child, whether or not we are aware of it. A lesson was passed on to us by someone who we believed to be in charge or authori-tative in our life. This someone explained or said something we accepted to be the honest truth. We believed it then, and we continue to act on it now—consciously at times and subconsciously other times.

To begin tapping about a negative behavior or habit, start tapping on any acu-puncture point. Close your eyes, and ask yourself, "How is this habit serving me?" Once you have opened your session with prayer, you have given the Holy Spirit permission to tell you exactly what He thinks and exactly what you are thinking and feeling that lies underneath the behaviors.

That question of how a habit is serving you will often elicit negative feelings, both emotionally and physiologically. After tapping on these negative feelings, ask the Holy Spirit what those feeling remind you of. This will likely bring back a child-hood or young-adult memory or event. Tap and neutralize everything God just handed to you as an answer to that question. Tap on those emotions, and tap on everything you specifically feel about where you sense that emotion in your body regarding whatever memory the Holy Spirit just reminded you of, and tap about the specifics of the memory.

Once you have tapped every emotion you feel, re-evaluate once again what you are feeling in the present moment regarding the bad habit you want to change. If you find another physical or emotional feeling, repeat the steps until you have eliminated every single detail around whatever supports that ungodly habit. This tapping alone may eliminate the desire to continue with the unwanted behavior.

PAUL'S PREDICAMENT

Romans 7:14–25 reads in the Message, *"I can anticipate the response that is coming: 'I know that all God's commands are spiritual, but I'm not. Isn't this also your experience?' Yes. I'm full of myself—after all, I've spent a long time in sin's prison. What I don't understand about myself is that I decide one way, but then I act another, doing things I absolutely despise. So if I can't be trusted to figure out what is best for myself and then do it, it becomes obvious that God's command is necessary."*

Jesus Christ really is our answer, and the answer He has now given us at this time and in this place seems to be EFT. He can often break the chains of those sinful habits using the powerful tool of tapping.

This next step is useful for any habit or behavior that has you stuck—those habits you cannot control, such as those that Apostle Paul discusses in Romans. You can use this next step in addition to the previous suggestion or in lieu of it.

STEP ONE

Close your eyes, and picture yourself right now doing that awful habit that you so despise. Clearly picture it in all its sinfulness. Tap on any acupuncture point while you do this.

If you have never confessed this sin to your heavenly Father, do it right now. Tap while you confess. Feel into your heart. Is there a color or a feeling associated with this specific sin? Does the color or feeling change after your confession? There are no correct answers to the sensory or emotional feelings this process elicits. It's all your perception.

Ask yourself how you *feel* about that behavior at this present moment. What emotions are popping up in your head? How strong are they? Then attach SUDS numbers to these feelings. Again, zero means you feel nothing; ten means you feel completely out of control. What's your number?

Next, tap those emotions down to zero. Once the SUDS is a zero, stop tapping, take a deep breath, and ask yourself the same questions again while picturing that same bad habit in your head. Are the emotions truly gone? If the answer is yes, then add one more layer to the question by following the second step that follows.

If the emotions still exist, resume tapping on each emotion, while finding other earlier events that the emotions remind you of, until you have cleared them all or as many as it takes for the "generalization effect" to kick in. The generalization effect happens because we have "mirror neurons" in our body. While tapping, mirror neurons look for similar or associated events or memories to the one you are tapping on.[89] Most often, when the subconscious finds another memory, it neutralizes it, along with the memory you are presently tapping on. If you can truly say your SUDS is a zero, stop tapping, and then proceed to step two.

STEP TWO

Start tapping and picture the scene again. But now tell yourself, and feel into this, that you must do that behavior every minute of every day—24 hours a day, 7 days a week, for 365 days! What are you now feeling when you see yourself committing that sin or doing that behavior every hour of the day for the rest of your life? You cannot stop to eat, or go to work, or talk to your spouse. You are stuck doing this behavior forever. Do any other emotions come up? If so, tap each one away. If no additional emotions surface, you may well have neutralized half the situation. Stop tapping.

STEP THREE

Start tapping and picture yourself again doing that habit. But now tell yourself, and feel your body's reaction to this as you say this preferably out loud, "I cannot do _____ ever again." You fill in the blank with your own personal habit or sin. What feelings does that statement elicit in you? On rare occasions, you may feel nothing but relief. But in most cases, the opposite emotion will flare up. It may be a feeling of sadness— a deep, deep sadness that you can no longer do something you had once

---

89   Church, *The Genie in Your Genes*, 200–201.

convinced yourself that you enjoyed. Be honest. Tap those emotions down to as close to zero as you can.

TEST IT

Test your tapping work. One more time, re-picture the scene, but this time tell yourself you will never, never be able to do anything remotely like this habit for fear it will trigger you back into this behavior. What feelings does that draw out of you? If they are negative, once again tap those feelings down to a zero.

One emotion that few people consider negative is the feeling of excitement. We usually think of it as something positive, as in we are excited for Christmas morning, or we anticipate a much-needed vacation. Those situations of excitement are positive and healing, but what about the excitement that comes with anticipation of doing something immoral or illegal?

WHY WE LOVE WHAT WE HATE

People trapped in immoral or illegal behavior often feel excited. That excitement is a mixture of their personal neurochemicals that began when the sinful behavior started years before. Often this is what traps us. We blame the enemy when much of it is our own physiology trapping us because our bodies release endorphins and dopamine, chemicals that make us feel good and entice us to repeat the sinful behavior because it gives us a sense of physical pleasure. We enjoyed doing whatever negative behavior we did, and now we are addicted to that pleasurable feeling of excitement, sinning again and again.

EFT can be a wonderful tool to root out and excise those immoral behaviors. If you feel excitement for a sinful behavior, SUDS that excitement, and then tap it down to a zero.

You may want to ask the Holy Spirit to find a couple of earlier examples of when that excitement and its accompanying neurochemical reaction began. When He gives those earlier memories to you, tap all the emotions out of those memories like you would tap anything else in your life. These memories happened to us, most likely, prior to the age of 25. At age 25 our adult brain is fully developed. Until that time, others can still easily influence us.

HOW THIS WORKS

The story that follows will help illustrate more clearly the approach I just outlined. A client I'll name Sally asked for help to tap because her past sexual behaviors were beginning to creep up on her again. She was extremely fearful she would once again fall to the temptations of the enemy, returning to old promiscuous actions, ones of which she had repented. She had remained celibate ever since that confession. But something was once again triggering those old desires and temptations.

Sally and I had previously tapped on many parts of her childhood memories, dismantling many of those younger events, freeing up other parts of her life. Embarrassed by this new development, I had her tapping right off the bat from the moment I detected something shameful-sounding amiss in her voice. We were tapping over the phone.

Sally explained to me that a new man had entered her life recently in an unexpected way. It shouldn't have surprised her because she had been praying for God to bring someone special into her life. What did surprise her, however, were the extreme sexual feelings she had for this man I'll name John. She felt if John suggested anything sexual, she would simply succumb to his requests without a second thought. Sally understood their behavior was already too flirtatious for this early point in a possible relationship. Simply put, she wanted to jump into the sack with John right here, right now, regardless of the consequences.

However, she knew her feelings were out of control, and they were most definitely sinful. She was ashamed of herself, but that didn't lessen the physical desire and emotional excitement she was experiencing.

I had her tapping the entire time she was explaining her problem to me, in her matter-of-fact, frank manner. God created us as sexual beings, and we all understand how our sexuality can easily get out of control. Those emotions push us around, shoving us in directions we know are immoral, and then leave us with the feeling God is very disappointed with us.

Sally couldn't have agreed more, and so we tapped on all those points of view, and on every emotion she was feeling. One important point I revealed to Sally, which she had not previously considered, was although she had repented of her past sexual actions, it had never entered her mind that her sexually explicit thoughts were "lust."

"Bingo!" she exclaimed when I said those words the Holy Spirit put into my mind to speak. I tapped with her as she confessed those lustful thoughts of what she wanted to do with this new man in her life. Our time ran out for our appointment, so we "sneaked away"[90] with tapping statements like, "Even though there is more to this sexual issue, God has it all under control, and I must yield to His precepts." Later, after I prayed for Sally, as I often do for my clients, some interesting follow-ups came through.

I suggested to her that she do the exact exercise I just explained here in these previous pages. I instructed her to tap on both sides of her feelings and pull out the emotions around, "The next time I see John I will simply give up and give in no matter what and go to bed with him" and "I will never, ever again be able to have any sexual relations with anyone the rest of my life. God will never give me a life partner."

She had extremely strong emotions around both sides of those statements. Many times, seemingly opposite emotions are actually the exact same emotion. Why? The reason is both extremes present different aspects of the core issue. Each emotion holds a different piece of the puzzle and a different meaning to the subconscious where those neurochemicals were first conceived.

We must always look at our behavior with an eye to what God thinks about it. That means before we tap away our feelings around our sinful behavior in an attempt to change our habits, we must always repair the vertical relationship we have with our Father in Heaven by confessing and repenting of our sin. 1 John 1:9 in the Message reads, "On the other hand, if we admit our sins—make a clean breast of them—he won't let us down; he'll be true to himself. He'll forgive our sins and purge us of all wrongdoing."

---

90   An EFT technique that we use at the end of a session when appointment time runs out if any intensity is left in the issue that is being worked on.

THE REST OF THE STORY

Sally continued her follow-up email to outline a very long list of childhood memories around an accidental health problem she had and how all the circumstances around it ended up sexualized to her from a very early age.

Yes, she learned sexuality early, ingraining her mind's neurochemicals, probably learning at a young age how to use her sexuality to get what she wanted and needed in life. She got attention from adults in childhood in a sexual way through medical treatments and procedures. No one sexually abused her, but her sex organs got her a lot of attention. Her subconscious has never forgotten that attention and excitement.

Sally's early sexuality is not serving her adult needs now, and is only dragging her into trouble. She understands this behavior must be modulated in order to keep her out of sexual temptation. Thankfully, God has given Sally a self-help skill to do just that. Shortly after tapping, Sally ended the relationship with John. This is a privilege and honor to help a fellow sister in Christ demolish sinful behaviors that are interfering in her relationship with Jesus and holding her back from experiencing His wonderful blessings for her.

EFT can help us become the best version of ourselves. When we are healed from the pain and issues of our past, we are able to live into the fullness of freedom God wants for us. What a gift!

CHAPTER 15

Big Traumas

Up to this point, we have discussed a lot about emotions and negative events in our lives. Now, I want to delve deeper into memories that are so impactful, we Emotional Freedom Techniques practitioners call them "Big T Traumas." These events make a huge impact in your life and can affect you in one of two polar opposite ways. Either you remember every single detail of the event, or you may virtually not remember anything about the event, except knowing something awful happened and it changed everything.

These Big T Traumas include deaths, accidents, abuse—anything that happened out of the blue, suddenly, surprisingly—and you felt completely helpless and hopeless. You probably thought you were about to die. That is trauma. Most significant are the aspects of feeling *helpless* and *hopeless*. You had no resources, nowhere to turn, or no one to turn to for assistance. You felt doomed.

This type of trauma often leads to post-traumatic stress-like symptoms. It's an awful situation with an equally dreadful feeling. Many times these are the memories or events we bury deep within our subconscious because we never again want to think about them or deal with them. Sadly, the effects of these situations usually haunt us until the day we die—unless we apply an inner healing tool such as Emotional Freedom Techniques to them.

Dissociation may result from these traumas. Dissociation is the forgetting and burying of one or more details of the event. The event is so painful and scary, we simply forget it ever happened or we forget pieces of it. We don't make a conscious decision to do that. Our subconscious mind does it for us, particularly if we are young and vulnerable—especially children younger than age seven. But sometimes, the subconscious mind also hides memories of traumas that happen in later life.[91]

In dissociated memories, the event may also be disconnected from any emotional feelings. The hurt person simply goes numb, feeling nothing about the memory, and sometimes nothing about life in general. For example, when I talk with Christians about EFT, I often hear them tell me this or that terrible thing happened to them, but they are fine because "God has taken care of it."

I certainly will never disagree God can take care of anything He so chooses. I do have to admit, however, I push these Christian brethren just a little bit sometimes. I want them to explain how God took care of it. I'm a details lady; I want to know precisely how the healing happened.

I like to ask if and how the event still plays out in their lives. It really never matters which answer they give me, though. Some say the memory doesn't bother them at all, or one thing or another is still a wee bit painful about the incident.

If the incident no longer bothers them, are they truly healed, or have they dissociated the memory? If the memory still bothers them on any level, I suggest that tapping might benefit them. Remember, anything that gives you a negative physiological feeling is tapping material. If a memory crosses your mind that makes your heart race (or any other physical feeling), it is having a negative impact on your body by raising your cortisol level, blood sugar, blood pressure, and a myriad of other chemical stressors that harm your health.

HEALING REGRET

I worked with a 50-something-year-old client a few years back I'll name June. She is a fellow Christian, and we were tapping about her excessive drinking. June had no control over it and feared becoming an alcoholic. As we tapped, her memory of an abortion she had in college surfaced.

I asked her to tap and to tell me what happened. She gave me a few details around the abortion then quickly told me God had forgiven her, and the abortion no longer bothered her.

---

91   Van der Kolk, *The Body Keeps the Score*, 66–68.

This gave me the opening I hoped for. This is where I often "push" with clients. My job as a Christian EFT practitioner is to know which buttons to press. When the Holy Spirit opens the door, I usually go for it!

After ascertaining my Christian client had asked God for forgiveness and had repented of the deed she did in the past, I asked her to tune into that past event, thinking about it today, telling me exactly how she feels *now* looking back at it. This is important. **Tapping must be used on how we feel today about a past event**, not how we felt when the event happened.

I asked June to think about that abortion 32 years ago. I asked, "What do you feel about it and where do you feel it?" As June tapped, I could see the look on her face change. She was beginning to realize even though she thought the emotions around the abortion were gone, they weren't.

She looked up at me, a bit surprised, and said, "I feel something in my heart."

"What is it?" I asked."

She answered, "I don't know, but I think it might be regret."

That is all we needed. It was exactly what I was looking to discover. Often, many Christians confess the sin they committed, but few realize that without tapping away the physiological effects of the sin, their total healing may not come. In their head, they *know* they're forgiven, but in their heart, they have yet to experience the *feeling* of forgiveness. This is what tapping can deliver.

The sin, with all of the intertwined neurochemicals, is still caught in and stored within the cells of the body. God certainly has forgiven them, but because of how He created our neurology, the effects still exist in the body. It is those effects that are still running the stress physiology that science now knows is so very damaging to us.

I continued with June by asking, "So on the scale of 1 to 10, how high is your regret over that abortion?"

"An 8," June answered. And with that, she began to sob.

You see, we walk right into God's outstretched arms and His immediate forgiveness the moment we confess, and He even forgets the sin. Scripture clearly tells us this in Hebrews 8:12, "For I will forgive their wickedness and will remember their sins no more." Confessed and gone, all in a nanosecond!

What many Christians forget is God doesn't always remove the effects or results of our emotion-filled sins within our cells, even though He has forgiven the sin. The eternal consequences have been ameliorated, but the earthly consequences aren't always so quick to go, if they go at all.

Sometimes, the effects of our sins stay in our minds and bodies for the rest of our lives. It is likened to a person who is sentenced to decades in prison for something they are now sorry for and have confessed. The consequences of their actions, however, don't change—the person is incarcerated. God has forgiven them, but still the prison walls remain.

That is exactly what happened with June. She knew God had forgiven her, but she still felt terrible about murdering her baby, and she still felt trapped in an emotional prison. While tapping, she realized she was carrying that pain in her heart.

Physiologically, such circumstances can have implications decades later. According to epigenetics, if we carry an emotional event in our heart, we increase the risk of it manifesting itself as cardiac problems in the future. Remember, the subconscious is literal. It will take our words as we spoke them and implant them into our physiology.

If condemnation is associated with the feelings, it very well may be the enemy doing the condemning, keeping us trapped in the thoughts that God could never forgive such a heinous crime. However, we know there is no condemnation for those who are in Christ Jesus (Romans 8:1).

Remember, the Holy Spirit convicts (John 16:8). It is the accuser of the brethren who condemns (Revelation 12:10). Conviction leads to repentance; condemnation leads to death (John 10:10).

Condemnation eats at us from the inside as we wonder, worry, and mull the "what ifs" of our lives forever. We never move forward. We feel stuck as if someone bolted down our feet to the cement sidewalk. We go nowhere with God.

Always be careful and investigate a bit further when someone says God fixed something completely. Never doubt God to be able to heal it, but make sure nothing was left behind underneath the event—a lingering negative emotion around what took place.

Taking this extra step is the stuff a joyful life can be made from—making sure all underlying negativity is gone—and can bring on the abundance of peace Jesus blessed us with in John 14:27, "Peace I leave with you; my peace I give you. I do not give to you as the world gives. Do not let your hearts be troubled and do not be afraid."

Tapping all those individual feelings and eliminating the charge around them can lead to that peace we all crave in our hectic lives. This is the peace of Christ, knowing we are loved, forgiven, and saved.

> June and I tapped on her level 8 SUDS of her "regret." We tapped and we prayed, giving the negative emotion to God, nailing it on the cross with Jesus. It took about 15 minutes of prayer and tapping to undo the decades of pain June had stuffed in her heart over that abortion, something she didn't even realize was there.
>
> Once I saw her face soften and knew God had truly released the regret, I asked her, "How do you feel?"
>
> "Much better," she replied.
>
> "Praise God. So now, let's once again tap on your collarbone point and feel into that day you aborted your baby. How high is your regret right now?" I asked June.
>
> She tapped for 30 seconds with her head bowed, appearing prayerful. She looked up at me and answered, "It's gone!" Her grin began in earnest as she continued, "I never realized that feeling was even there until now, after it's gone!"

FREEDOM FROM SADNESS

The story of Betty is another example of EFT healing. Betty is a strong believer. God is her everything! He'd brought her through thick and thin, including a rough childhood and a terrible accident that led to disability.

When on the phone, we were finally ready to tap, but she had no idea what to tap on.

After explaining how EFT works and how we plant our emotions somewhere in our bodies, I asked Betty to do a "body scan." A body scan is done by closing one's eyes and slowly feeling down through the body from tip of the head to the bottom of the feet, just relaxing, and noticing if anything at all feels hot, cold, tense, tight, lumpy, or simply out of place. The feeling can be absolutely anything out of the ordinary.

It's fairly rare when clients don't notice something odd about how they feel. Betty was no exception. She realized the base of her neck felt odd, but she couldn't describe the feeling. Finally, she decided the closest feeling was an itchy sensation underneath the skin.

After opening with prayer, we began to tap on that "itchy sensation at the base of my neck." As with so many other Christian clients, Betty pipes up, "Well, I don't know if this is anything because God has healed me of it and I've forgiven my husband and everything is good."

"You've forgiven him of what?" I asked.

"Oh, I told you, didn't I? Brian had that affair 20 years ago and it near killed me." Betty spoke matter-of-factly.

This sounded like dissociation: A big trauma happened to us, but we have no feelings at all around the event. It's an emotionless memory. If the memory is neutralized after tapping, then that is a good thing. But if we have simply stuffed the memory somewhere in our body and are no longer feeling it, then it's dissociation. Remember, it is the tapping itself, stimulating those acupuncture points, that discharges the emotion by telling our brain structures we are safe.

I continued, "So, thinking now about that affair of Brian's, what do you feel and where do you feel it?" I asked.

"I guess I still feel some sadness about it, that he did it at all. There is something scratching around in my throat as I think about it," Betty told me.

"Right now, tune into that sadness in your throat, and give me a number on that scale of 1–10. How sad are you? One is you aren't sad and 10 is you are really, really sad," I explained.

"This surprises me," she told me, "I'm a 7. Is that pretty high?"

"It is definitely high enough to tap on, so let's give it to God once and for all," I replied.

Betty and I tapped around that sadness for a while until her SUDS was a 1. She couldn't believe how much better she felt now that her throat no longer itched and scratched. At the end of the session, she said to me, "You know, I've wanted to tell God to take that sadness away for a long time, but I never felt I had a right to ask, since He gave me my husband back. No wonder my throat itched. Those words wanted out!"

FINALLY. AMEN, SISTER!

Sometimes, bad things happen in our lives because of something we did to invite the negative consequences. Other times, people foist events on us, but we still have committed sin because we are angry about the problem, and we allow it to lead to hate, resentment, grief, and many other negative emotions. Anger itself is not a sin, but it becomes sin if we continue to dwell on it (Ephesians 4:26). We can't let anger run our lives, nor should we bury it deep inside because it is too painful to deal with.

Ecclesiastes 7:9 warns us "anger lodges in the heart of fools." Let that not be us! EFT can be a practical tool we use to access these hidden emotions of our inner man. To get deep inside and unbury the hurt, dislodge the anger and free ourselves from the chains of emotional pain. Through EFT, we can tap into the freedom of Heaven as God's Spirit heals us from the inside out, transforming us—thought by thought, feeling by feeling, from glory to glory—into the image of Jesus (2 Corinthians 3:18). Hallelujah!

CHAPTER 16

Generational Curses

You know the old adage, "If Momma ain't happy, ain't no one happy"? Up until recently, that was the *modus operandi* in my house, just as it had been the *way of operating* in my childhood home. Families have generational ways of doing things. Some of it is cultural and ethnic. None of that is bad in its strictest sense, but when a familial behavior is destructive or sinful, the child in the household knows no better and actually believes it is the moral way to act. Thus begin the problems.[92]

My unhappiness was all due to my own personal internal "demons" running my life. I had somehow applied a perfectionist rule of order on myself, and I expected every single person on the planet to jump to my tune. It was pure self-absorbed behavior running amok in my life—perfectionist traits I learned from my mom.

Does anyone else have this problem? Do you feel constantly on edge, like you want to jump out of your skin most of the time? Silly, little things seem to send you over the edge where you find yourself flying off the handle about something that 10 minutes later embarrasses you to no end? You realize you are out of control much of the time, but no matter what you do or what you say to yourself, nothing ever changes. It's a near helpless, hopeless feeling that life is a series of calamities, most of them minor, but you find yourself reacting like Chicken Little—the sky is falling!

Once again, I'm going to tell on myself. This used to be my behavior. It was maddening because I know the reactions I had to small things in life were proportionally too much. Small incident = big reaction. In Emotional Freedom Techniques,

---

92 Church, *The Genie in Your Genes*, 260.

we call this a "disproportional response." Actually, this reaction can go either way, as illustrated by the story of June's abortion in the previous chapter. That was a big problem with little reaction—the opposite of my small problem with a big response.

EXTREME REACTIONS

Examples of my behavior: going near ballistic if the toilet paper roll was on backwards in the holder or items in the refrigerator weren't lined up just right according to how I thought they should be. God help anyone who messed up my own self-imposed rule of order! Occasionally, I could hold my wrath if my day had gone well. But if I had an unnervingly busy day, I simply lost it, yelling and screaming at whomever I suspected ruined my self-conceived idea of how neatness should be. Frankly, now after learning EFT, I found I had a lot of apologizing to do!

Why did I go off on anyone within hearing proximity when the mailbox flag wasn't put up when an outgoing letter was inside? Why did every throw rug in the house have to sit just so upon the floor? Why did towels in the linen closet have to line up like little tin soldiers ready for a mission? Why did a glob of escaped toothpaste on a mirror bother me so badly? Why did I flip out if the kitchen cupboard doors were left hanging open, or someone slammed them a wee bit harder than I thought was needed to shut them? What in the world was fueling this chronic, obsessive behavior? Sadly, it wasn't just stressing me internally; I imposed the stress on everyone around me—just as I perceived life to be when I was growing up.

Looking back in a saner moment, what selfishness! I've done much personal tapping work along with confession and repentance on these memories. I highly encourage you do the same when the Holy Spirit helps you see through all the behavioral errors you have committed. What a gracious God we have Who is patient with us until such healing time as this.

So, how did I come to find myself in such a highly triggered behavioral state? Am I just one of those perfectionistic types of people? We often assume behaviors like this are just our personality.

While we can excuse our behavior as just that—perfectionism—it rarely serves us or anyone around us, particularly children who watch this behavior day in and day out, emulating their parents' actions. Order and discipline are appropriate, but excessive reactions around order and discipline are not a good thing at all. It creates stress for the obsessive thinker and for those on the receiving end of that mindset.

Perfectionism tends to have some underlying thought process bound up in it. That thought process often has to do with a core issue like, "I'm not good enough" or "I don't deserve," or a feeling of powerlessness. Those insidious thought mechanisms can destroy lives because, eventually, when perfectionism isn't attainable the person often gives up, falling into despair and depression. Physical issues can often be the end result of this desire to do everything just right. Many people who claim "Type A" personalities can be those with perfectionistic tendencies. They strive until they drop from the stress and strain of the endless effort. Suicide can be the result when the person realizes he can never achieve the perfect end.

For the rest of us who carry around over-reactive behaviors, this is one of those epigenetic familial tendencies. These are not true genetic disturbances, but learned family tendencies. As a child grows up in a family, he carefully watches parental reactions to everything happening within that unit. The child comes to understand that whatever is being said or done is *how* things *should* be said or done.

WHOSE TRUTH?

Children learn their "truth" from the adults around them. The closer the relational affinity, the more these learned actions mean to a child. Any adult who a child looks up to for love and support is the adult whose every word or action will imprint on that child. If the words or actions are positive, a positive outlook is planted in that child's mind. If those actions and words are negatively based or functionally out of order, the child still imprints that behavior as an appropriate way to act. Once learned it becomes the child's way of acting, and they carry that exhaustive behavior right into adulthood, often teaching it to their children.

I learned to be picky about how I handled chores around the house from my Mom. That's the person most children learn from. I'm not trying to be hard on moms, but they do spend the majority of child-rearing time with the kids. If Mom isn't secure in her own life, that insecurity easily gets passed onto the children. If Mom imposes almost impossible standards, the children then go on to demand the same from others in their adult lives. Those issues get handed down generation after generation. And so does the stress and accompanying anxiety, physical problems, and illnesses. These are learned coping mechanisms.

OF MICE AND MEN

A study at Emory University by Kerry Ressler states[93]:

"Ressler's lab at Yerkes is following up on some of these ideas in powerful mouse models of epigenetic transfer of fear across generations.

Ressler and fellow researcher Brian Dias trained mice to become afraid of an odor by pairing exposure to the odor with a mild electric shock. They then measured how much the animal startled in response to a loud noise alone, and then in conjunction with the odor.

Surprisingly, they found that the naïve adult offspring of the sensitized mice also startled more in response to the particular odor than one parent had learned to fear, despite the fact that they had never been exposed to the odor/shock combination.

In addition, the younger mice were more able to detect small amounts of that particular odor.

A third generation of mice also inherited this reaction, as did mice conceived through in vitro fertilization with sperm from males sensitized to the smell.

These offspring were not more anxious in general; in separate experiments not involving odors, Dias found that the mice were not more afraid to explore the bright, elevated areas of a maze.

Dias also discovered that the DNA from the sperm of the smell-sensitized father mice is altered. This is an epigenetic alteration, found not in the letter-by-letter sequence of the DNA but in its packaging or chemical modifications.

Knowing how the experiences of parents influence their descendants helps us understand psychiatric disorders that may have a transgenerational basis and possibly to design therapeutic strategies, Ressler says."

---

93   You may read the full article at http://emorymedicinemagazine.emory.edu/issues/2014/spring/features/the-anatomy-of-fear/

If mice can "learn" behaviors they never personally experienced, how much deeper does this resonate within us humans who God created in the most exquisite detail?

Epigenetic or environmental changes are biological markers on DNA that modify gene expression without altering the gene strands themselves. Researchers have found that many environmental factors including trauma, stress, and diet can activate epigenetic changes. Over-reactions from parental sources can be stress or even trauma if it is consistent and long-term. Stress activates these DNA markers which then lead to diseases.[94]

> "The science of epigenetics, (meaning control above genetics) studies the molecular mechanisms by which environment controls gene activity. It has established that a variety of environmental influences (e.g., nutrition, stress, emotions) can modify genes without changing their basic blueprint and this modification can be passed on to future generations."[95]

Epigenetic changes can switch disease genes on and off at will. Protein sheaths around the DNA "express" themselves, opening up the DNA to disease, causing damage. Bruce Lipton's statement "DNA does not control biology," says it all.[96]

Our DNA is easily damaged, and we know this damage happen tens of thousands of times a day in our bodies, and most of it is repaired but, occasionally, some of the damage goes unrepaired.[97]

Good parenting, including maternal-child bonding, is one of the biggest health improvement activities a parent can do for their children. Love and attention tends to keep these protein sheaths from expressing themselves, exposing the DNA to damage. Lifestyle changes in nutrition and exercise also improve these genetic markers, but the stable emotional component generates the most help in keeping a person healthy during a lifetime.[98]

---

94   Mate, *When the Body Says NO*, 229.
95   Lipton, *The Biology of Belief*, 2005, 67–68.
96   Ibid., 2008, 43.
97   www.intechopen.com/books/new-research-directions-in-dna-repair/dna-damage-dna-repair-and-cancer
98   This short video clip shows scientifically how DNA is exposed to damage https://vimeo.com/20064633

No parent decides he will be the world's worst parent; however, parents give a child only what they themselves know, were taught, or what they have experienced.[99]

If all a parent knows is war with its accompanying fear and terror emotions around those experiences, that is precisely what the parent is going to pass on to the child. If a parent knew nothing but hunger during childhood, those beliefs and habits around food will most certainly be taught to the child.

Several studies clearly underscore how this type of emotional pain is passed through the generations.[100]

> "The Centers for Disease Control (CDC) maintains that 85% of all diseases are caused by emotion. The health problems we are facing now, and the diseases that may be lurking in our futures, are a direct manifestation of the emotional traumas we have lived through and how we have chosen to react to them."[101]

THIRD AND FOURTH GENERATIONS

I believe all of the issues discussed here are part of the package of generational curses discussed in the Old Testament, passed down to the third and fourth generations of those who disobeyed God (Exodus 34:6–7).

When we see families with generation after generation of alcoholism, we ask, "What is going on?" It isn't inherited in the strictest sense, but it is inherited in an epigenetic sense. The children of an alcoholic parent learn how to control and show their emotions or to stuff those emotions from that parent. They also learn that expressing their feelings is not acceptable, so they follow the addicted parent's lead and "numb out" in an attempt to feel nothing at all. The children learn the alcoholic patterns from the parent. Drugs are also used to numb out our unwanted

---

99 Church, *The Genie in Your Genes*, 251.
100 Here are a couple examples of the multiple dozens of studies available:
    www.scientificamerican.com/article/descendants-of-holocaust-survivors-have-altered-stress-hormones/
    http://indiancountrytodaymedianetwork.com/2015/05/28/trauma-may-be-woven-dna-native-americans-160508
    http://forward.com/culture/318509/is-jewish-anxiety-no-laughing-matter/
101 http://undergroundhealthreporter.com/emotional-healing-eft/#ixzz3ncAPiXkj

feelings. When children are traumatized, they act out for attention or numb out by exhibiting undesirable behaviors because the pain is too much to endure.[102]

> "The brain's adaptation to chronic fear and anger can trigger permanent changes in hormone levels, which may be picked up by the genes and passed on, (e.g., generations may become successively more aggressive)."[103]

Tapping, we now believe, can be used to eliminate the emotional underpinnings of a harsh childhood, or to help eliminate emotional reactions we learned from parents who learned them from their parents, for generations. In this way addictions can often be brought under control.

As mundane as my irritability was, I continued to dwell on and become upset because the socks were inside out in the dirty clothes hamper, or if the boys hadn't emptied their pockets before tossing their jeans in the washer. I was literally killing myself with stress. Where had I learned that such details were the most important I had to focus on? You know the answer. I learned it from my own mom.

So I was affected on a cellular level because the traits I inherited from my mother was expressed in an unhealthy way, and I was also affected simply because of my mother's behavior that I witnessed, was subjected to, and eventually modeled.

Now, in the big picture, such tiny obsessive stress should be nothing; however, if I dwelled on those silly little things in life, can you imagine what I did with my big worries and worse behaviors?

I learned the art of worry, irritability, and obsession in childhood—all a part of environmental familial genetics. I was taught those things were important. And, in all honesty, we were verbally punished if we didn't comply in making sure our sheets were tucked in properly, come in from recess promptly and on time, or the bathroom light wasn't turned off immediately upon exiting.

Whatever a parent or even a teacher thought was important became important to me also. Boots lined up in a straight line in the entry way, handwriting correctly formed on a letter, or a term paper turned in sans typos all were done to avoid a harsh word, but all that behavior caused an immense amount of childhood stress.

---

102 Van der Kolk, *The Body Keeps the Score*, 67.
103 Karr-Morse, *Ghosts from the Nursery*, 167–168.

I strove for a perfection I couldn't achieve, and all of it caused an outside irritability toward everyone around me when I couldn't manage to accomplish in good order what I was told to do. I fussed, fumed, and became more and more angry, lashing out at friends or siblings when I felt near ready to explode, sending the pain further down the chain to the younger children. I couldn't lash out at adults for fear of more discipline.

REALITY CHECK

When I became an adult, I thought my situation was simply the way everyone did things. Everything properly lined up, in order, without any mistakes. I was stunned to find out other people didn't lash out at one another constantly. I grew up thinking everyone behaved like I was taught. Amazingly, it took learning EFT to realize I was out of line with my expectations, and over the edge in reacting to simple mistakes in life.

After I began to tap on a regular basis, God released these unhealthy, fine-tuned behaviors in me. He graciously pointed out I had no need for perfection, nor would I ever attain it, as that was Jesus' job. He also released the underlying chemical addiction I had around those behaviors, lowering my cortisol level that was triggered by my amygdala every time I saw something out of order. It all was hardened into place within my neurochemistry. Tapping undoes both the subconscious beliefs around a behavior and the chemical trap we find ourselves caught in.

Forgiveness for myself and others came rushing in as those early perfectionistic tendencies and memories were neutralized while tapping. Oh, I still like the house neatly in order, but does it really matter if at times piles of mail accumulate or a cupboard door gets left ajar? Not really. God now has more important jobs for me to do!

By tapping, I unplugged neurologically those behaviors that were leading me into health issues later in life. And the real beauty of all of this is — we can often still heal years later from all the earlier damage we inadvertently did to ourselves. Thankfully, God created us with such balance that as soon as our cortisol level drops, healing DHEA levels should return to normal, bringing the immune system back on-line to a healthy homeostasis once again.

No one can live in those high states of learned stress and irritability forever and stay healthy. EFT can return us to better states of health. God has given us EFT to help us live more productive and happier lives. If you find yourself stressed because of some inherited behavior, ask God to help you release it to Him.

Tap and go back into the memories of your childhood, allowing the power of the Holy Spirit to break those neural connections and set you free today. Jesus was always by your side, even as a child, so look to see Him there with you. What was He saying and what was He doing? Let His perspective replace the painful picture in your heart. Let His joy replace your sadness and His strength replace your weakness, and tap it in.

SUB-SECTION FOUR:
Tapping Into Positive Emotions

CHAPTER 17

Can We Tap Positively?

The dynamic between Christians and Emotional Freedom Techniques presents one consistent problem: Christians predominantly want to tap on the positives in life! Somehow, they think that by positively repeating again and again what they want, it will come true. Perhaps, if God hears them often enough, He will answer their prayer and give them their heart's desire.

EFT tapping is done from the negative perspective. In tapping, we are allowed to whine, complain, moan and groan, rant, and wail. We tap exactly how we feel or see the problem. For once, stating our troubles negatively is a good thing – as long as we are tapping while talking about the issues.

When wanting to tap, many Christians tell me, "Oh, I can't say such negative things. They will come true." Exactly! So I retort, "But it's what you're thinking anyway!" You attract precisely what you are thinking or saying (Proverbs 18:21; Matthew 12:37). Jesus said, "According to your faith let it be done to you" (Matthew 9:29).

A basic principle of EFT is this: All negative thinking eventually becomes our reality through perception. Your positive thoughts are not your problem; your negative thoughts are.

The more you think a thought—positive or negative—the more entrenched that thought becomes. Your subconscious mind will believe anything you tell it to believe. When I think of this concept, I think of "mind-control." In a sense, that is exactly what tapping is: controlling our mind in the positive. However, you are currently controlling your *OWN* mind with your own *NEGATIVE* self-talk.

MIND CHATTER

Most self-talk is negative. We tell ourselves how stupid we are, how ugly we are, how unloved we are, how fat we are, how undeserving we are, what a reject we are, how unlikeable we are, and on and on. We probably have hundreds of such learned sayings. And every single time you think or say a habitual negative thought, you entrench it, you embed it, you dig the belief further and further into your neural pathways!

Pay close attention to what comes out of your mouth. Listen to yourself talk. You will often find yourself saying repetitive negative comments about yourself either out loud or under your breath. Those are tappable statements. Questions to ask yourself are: "Who told me that?" "Where did I learn that comment?" Those questions often bring back specific memories of a time where you learned those limited beliefs. These can all be tapped on.

I mentioned before that for every hour we think a thought, whether it is positive or negative, we double the neural pathways to that thought.[104] "So as we think, it is," is a paraphrase of Proverbs 23:7. Obviously, Scripture is true—whatever we dwell on is what we become. If we dwell on how much God loves us, then that becomes our normal prevailing thought. If we dwell on how badly our parents hurt us, then that perception and experience will run our emotional life.

OUR PERCEPTIONS CREATE OUR REALITY

According to John McCrone, as quoted in *The Genie in Your Genes,* our brain has 1,000 trillion synaptic connections to move along all the learned information of our lives.[105] Eric Kandel, M.D., winner of the Nobel Prize in Medicine in 2000, "discovered that when new memories are established, the number of synaptic connections in the sensory neurons stimulated jumped to around 2600, a doubling of its previous count of 1,300. Unless the initial experience was reinforced, however, the number of connections dropped back to 1,300 within three weeks."[106]

To repeat, positive self-statements aren't the problem; negative ones are! And sadly, none of the negative beliefs other people project to you may be true. It is a simple matter of someone else's opinion about you, or his own negative self-talk being projected onto you. Once your subconscious mind hears what you or oth-

104 Church, *The Genie in Your Genes*, 100.
105 Ibid., 151.
106 Ibid., 99.

ers say, it takes that "perception" and makes it your reality. You become what you think or say you are!

Therefore, your subconscious "says" to itself, "You say you are fat, so I will make you fat," and you begin to gain weight for no explainable reason. "You say you are ugly, so I will cover your face with pimples and eczema, making you look and feel uglier," and your face breaks out, leaving you with no clue about what is going on—nor your doctor; and everything he prescribes doesn't help one little bit. "You say you are stupid, so I will make sure your next job is so above your educational ability, you will look stupid when you cannot do it."

We often see these negative beliefs at work in children. Someone tells them how "stupid" they are, and we watch as the child slumps down in his seat with a pouty face only to absolutely refuse to try taking the science test. Note that the statement may be said by a peer, or the peer simply laughed, but the child's "perception" of the laugh means he is stupid. The child gets a "D" on the test, and the peer doing the taunting has just been proven correct in the child's mind. A neural pathway around, "I'm so stupid," has just been formed, and the educational troubles have just commenced. It can truly be that simple for lifelong problems to begin! And these early thoughts can continue to hold you back as an adult.

Tapping, however, can help you to eliminate these patterns, getting to the bottom of why you think these negative thoughts about yourself. God has bigger and better things planned for you than allowing you to wallow in these perceptions, and that is all they tend to be—perceptions. Another real-life example illustrates this process perfectly.

THE PINK "F"

This story, written in her own words, is from Shauna, an R.N. friend of mine, who plans to become a certified Christian EFT Practitioner.

For most of his life, my son Scott has struggled academically. He's a wonderfully intelligent, soft-spoken, quiet young man who always had to work hard to get through school. He is smart; he is simply unable do well on tests. Early in grade school, he was tested for a learning disability, but the test results were normal. He continued for the next 12 years to battle his way through school. At times, it did feel like war! Until I learned EFT, I was at a complete loss as to how to help him. And, boy, do I wish I knew then what I know now!

Scott is now 20 years old. After working three part-time jobs, sometimes holding all three at once, and graduating from high school, he's returned to EMT school. His academic performance is okay, barely passing his tests, even after hours and hours of studying. He continues to struggle just to hang on.

Eighteen months ago, I learned EFT from Sherrie. Since then, I've had one session with Scott—it is difficult to pin down a 19-year-old to do something spiritual like tapping—to address his learning struggles.

We tapped about his general anxiety and negative self-esteem—his father left when Scott was 2 years old—and he seemed to do fine for a while thereafter.

Recently, Scott started to once again talk down on himself. I figured some other memory was surfacing in his subconscious, causing him more academic issues. I begged him for weeks to let me tap with him again. He has no extra time between school, studying, working a couple jobs, and his girlfriend!

After he generously took me out for Mother's Day breakfast (he really is a sweet kid), I pushed the issue of tapping with him a bit more over these school problems because on Monday morning he had his final EMT test. It was going to be a big part of his class grade. He had to do well on this final, or all his hard work will be for naught.

He allowed me 15 minutes for a session! We began to tap. Scott identified a few different feelings, but he really wasn't into the session at all. I tried a couple of different roundabout approaches, hoping he'd give me something specific to tap on. I was looking for an early in life event.

I asked him how he felt about school and his struggles. He said he was a failure and could never pass tests. He did great with hands-on practice assignments, but barely passed, sometimes failed, all the other tests this semester.

I asked if he felt the problem anywhere in his body. He said his eyes hurt from looking at the bright neon letters before his eyes.

I asked what part of that picture meant the most to him. This was the answer I was looking for, but I didn't realize it immediately.

"Pink letters," Scott answered.

I asked what those letters meant to him. His answer surprised me, "70% F." I realized then he was looking at big pink neon letters, stating he had failed—70% and an F!

I then asked him, "When was the first time the pink letters showed up?" He quickly replied, "First grade." He now had my interest piqued!

I asked him to close his eyes, picturing that first grade classroom, and describe it to me.

Not a problem for Scott. Off he went with the description of the classroom and how he failed his spelling test in first grade—70% was written in red ink on the paper!

My next question was another crucial key, "Who was your teacher?" At first he couldn't remember, but suddenly out of his mouth popped, "Ms. Huber."

"Ms. Huber? I don't remember any Ms. Huber! So, what is she doing in the classroom to you?" I asked.

Again, Scott's answer nearly floored me, "She told me that if I couldn't do first grade tests, I wouldn't be able to do anything in life either!"

Stunned, I inquired, "So, how do you feel about that statement now?"

Scott became pretty angry, so we tapped on the anger. I asked him if he had anything to say to Ms. Huber.

Well, my 20-year-old son had a lot to say to Ms. Huber, and I would have tolerated none of it if he were still in first grade, let me tell you! I told him to go ahead and say whatever it was he needed to say to her, out loud, or to himself. Of course, we were tapping the entire time through this short session.

It was out loud, and I heard a string of nasty swear words that, in reality, really were sweet to my ears, as crazy as that sounds. I now understood for the first time that his inability to take tests started 15 years ago.

My poor son had struggled all these years because of an inconsiderate statement spoken to him in first grade by a teacher who was probably having a bad day!

Is this the complete end to his academic problems? It very well may be, knowing now what I know about neuroscience. But time will tell. Today, however, I received a phone call that makes my Mother's Day of yesterday complete.

Scott was so excited to find out he earned an 88% on his final EMT test today—the test he was so very nervous about yesterday, and this is the BEST grade he has ever received on any test in a very long time. He was holding down a 78% grade in the class to date, and 81% was the best test score he received all semester. He needed an 81% final grade in class to remain in the program.

Had someone told me this story, and I was not the practitioner, I probably would have simply said, "'That's nice,'" and walked away.

I was the practitioner, and I saw exactly how EFT and tapping helped my son! And I am so excited for him, and I praise God He is watching over him better than I ever could, although I have done the very best to my ability.

I just hope Scott will allow me to do more tapping with him soon. At the end of our phone conversation, Scott said to me, "It's okay, Mom. God is watching over me!" He surely is by allowing me to learn EFT, so I could help my son undo that one damaging statement in first grade that set the tone for his entire academic life!

This is what we call a "one-minute wonder" in EFT, meaning the tapping was effected quickly. It doesn't usually happen quite this fast, but we are so grateful when it does!

ACKNOWLEDGING WHERE WE ARE TO GET TO WHERE WE'RE GOING

As we tap, using the set-up phrase of "Even though I have this problem (you state specifically your own problem here), God loves me and has a plan for my life (or your own version of an acceptance statement)," two things happen. First, we "expose" ourselves to the realities of what we think and what we believe to be true. Second, we offer ourselves to God's acceptance of us—just the way we are.

God does accept and love us how we are; however, He loves us too much to leave us that way. As we repent of our sins, confessing them to God Almighty, and tapping the emotions around those sins, the Lord can work miracles in our lives through the process of sanctification, making us more and more like Jesus. We can allow those sinful habits, thoughts, and behaviors to often melt away under His grace and mercy.

Negative tapping is like cleaning out a wound before applying antibiotic ointment and a clean bandage. None of us will ever bandage a dirty, unwashed wound and expect it to actually heal. Most likely, the wound will fester and become infected under its bandage.

It is no different with EFT. Your emotional wounds have been festering for years, maybe decades. In most cases, the festering has gotten worse and worse. This happens especially in post traumatic events—these problems rarely heal on their own without in-depth professional help.

Positive tapping, before you have completely tapped out every single negative thought and feeling surrounding a person or situation, is simply a pep talk, much like a sports rally. You get all energized and excited to make a change your life, then later your routine comes crashing back on you when someone says a negative comment, triggering you. Positive tapping—when it's the opposite of what you truly feel inside—is short-lived and will not give you any permanent results. We must first empty ourselves completely of the ungodly emotions and wrong thoughts. Only then can we make room for the positive feelings to take their place, allowing God to grow these new thoughts, renewing us in Him.

Negative tapping allows you to acknowledge the facts about the situation. Sometimes, it is the only time you will admit to yourself how badly you actually feel. Most times, we cannot allow ourselves that luxury because the impactful consequences could push us to the brink of ruining our will to live. Tapping while admitting the negative truth is a good thing! You are permitting your neural connections to actually consider changing for the better! You sever the negative thought bundle and can begin to build new positive thoughts.

That new positive neural bundle is tender, like a shoot of young grass, so it must be nourished and fed more positive thoughts—God's Word, prayer, and worship. This is one aspect of being transformed by the renewing of our mind (Romans 12:2).

Many times, the negative voices in our heads tell us one bad thing after another about ourselves. This is the programming into our subconscious that occurs when we are children. And as impressionable children, we are influenced by listening to the authority figures in our lives—authorities we had no choice but to listen to: parents, grandparents, teachers, neighbors, scout leaders, older siblings, and so on. We always believed they were smarter and knew more than we did. So if they said something negative about us, then it must be true. We internalized the negativity, making it our reality and our belief system…until we try tapping.

INTERVIEW ANXIETY

A client we'll call Darla came to me because her temporary job was ending, and she desperately wanted to find a good job in her specialty field of engineering computer programming. Darla wasn't a Christian, but tapping is available to people of all faiths and beliefs.

In our first session, we simply tapped globally on how she felt about her home details, her husband and his work, her children and their activities, and how she saw a new job fitting into everyone's lives and schedules, especially since she was nearly 100% responsible for their two young children.

A week later, I received an email from Darla telling me she had received a call from an engineering head hunter and she was on her third interview at a Fortune 500 company. She wanted to tap again with me as soon as possible because she was afraid of saying something wrong in an upcoming phone interview with the HR department of this new company.

At the next appointment, I used a "positive" statement to find the negative beliefs that lay underneath her subconscious thinking.

I asked Darla to give me all the exact details of what the perfect job would look like to her. She was precise indeed. She needed a job with little travel because she had 2 school-aged children at home, a specific yearly salary of $100,000, and full benefits including insurance, paid sick days and vacation time.

As we began tapping, I asked her if we could up the ante a bit around the perfect job.

"Like what?" she asked me.

"How about we tap for a higher salary and to allow your boss to let you work from home?" I countered.

Darla's husband often worked from home, and in the past she had expressed to me how desirable that would be for her, as it would allow her to balance childcare and work much better.

Darla was excited at that prospect, so I tossed out a higher salary of $125,000. What a great raise that would be, so Darla readily decided to tap on that better salary.

How did I start that tapping session? I asked Darla to imagine her new job exactly as we envisioned it—no travel (the Fortune 500 company told her in the first two interviews she would be flying to company headquarters out of state twice a week), full benefits, including 4 weeks of vacation a year, working from home, and a salary of over $10,000 a month.

My first question was, "Now, how much do you believe that job is yours and everything will be exactly as you want it to be, based on a scale of 0 to 10? Zero is you don't believe it and 10 is you totally believe the job is yours, with your name on it." Her answer was not at all surprising.

"I only believe it to be a 4," she told me.

I then asked, "So what is stopping you from getting that job tomorrow when HR phones you?"

She had a litany of reasons. The first was, "I'm afraid I will give them the wrong answer to a question and that will be the end of it." Darla's SUDS on that fear was high at an 8, so we tapped that to a zero.

Even though Darla isn't a Christian, we know God works in all of our lives, and His voice often comes as a spontaneous thought. As we were tapping on fear, Holy Spirit reminded Darla of an early childhood incident where intense fear interfered with a good outcome she had wanted. We tapped that incident to a zero, too.

I used a positive thought here to find the negative beliefs that were interfering with the subconscious. Was it me making something happen? No, it is all God! But God programmed us to allow things to happen in our lives based on what we *believe* will happen (Matthew 9:29). If we only believe negative things, the reality will be all negative. It's exactly how God created our neurology to work. If Darla believed she couldn't land that new job, there was a good possibility she wouldn't.

The session was almost 90 minutes long because Darla had multiple reasons why this new job prospect wouldn't work out. She would need to travel too much, and she couldn't leave the kids home alone because her husband was also frequently out of town for his job, the salary wouldn't be what she thought she was worth, and the company wouldn't offer health insurance, which she needed for her family.

After we tapped every single aspect that underpinned her negative reasons for not getting this job, the scale of her belief that the job was hers rose to a positive 8—using the SUE scale, Subjective Units of Experience, which is a positive scale unlike the SUDS, which is a negative scale. On positive beliefs we want the number to rise, as that indicates the client is believing the outcome can actually happen the way they wish it to happen.

Now that her SUE number was an 8, Darla was really comfortable in her thoughts that she could land this job with the upcoming morning interview. She knew her engineering skills were good, and she knew she could learn whatever new skills she needed to fulfill the new job requirements.

My last instructions to her were to continue tapping negatively on any new interfering beliefs that pop up over the ensuing couple of weeks. Often the negative beliefs come off in layers, like peeling an onion, and we must continue to tap down any new layer that gets exposed.

THE RESULTS

I knew Darla and her family were going on a week's vacation, so I didn't hear from her right away. She stopped by two weeks later to pick up a book, and she told me the rest of the story.

First, she admitted she was having so much fun with the children on vacation that she did no more tapping about her job issue, but she did indeed get the job. That was great news! She was extremely excited, thanking me profusely—though I had little to do with her obtaining the job except I did the "tapping process" with her. God is the generous One Who supplies for all our needs, to both the believer and the unbeliever!

Darla recounted the list of what she received in the new job deal – paid vacation and sick time, health insurance for her family, out of state travel only on occasion (not the twice a week requirement of the initial offering) and, most importantly, she could work from home. The company would set up her entire workspace at its expense, and she received a salary of $105,000 a year, $5,000 more than was offered before we tapped about her new job!

By removing the subconscious thought barriers to our desires within the will of God, our subconscious often helps to support allowing those exact things to happen. The Gospel in Matthew 17:20 tells us faith that is the size of a mustard seed is all the belief we need to move a mountain. In order for positive beliefs to develop, we must neutralize all negative thoughts and reasons around why we believe something cannot happen, allowing for a new positive thought to emerge within our neural pathways.

The most important rule: we must first undercut negative thoughts before we instill positive thoughts. Pretty flowers cannot flourish in a garden of tangled weeds. It is the same with the tangled negative neural pathways of our mind. Prune out the negative and plant in the positive. Through EFT, often the pruning allows the positive to grow on its own. After the negativity is eliminated, God then seeds our mind's garden with His own thoughts as we more fully experience the mind of Christ (1 Corinthians 2:16).

Remember: the only purpose for the use of the positive statement in this example was to uncover the negative thoughts held in the background of Darla's mind. We did not tap on the positive of, "This new Fortune 500 job is mine!"

Tapping on that positive statement would have been a waste of time. It would have yielded nothing good because Darla did not truly believe that statement (as indicated by her original 4 on the positive SUE scale). Only by tapping on her underlying negative thoughts were we able to bring that 4 up to an 8. I never want to leave a client with less than an 8 when I do positive tapping. A 9 or a 10 is even better!

TAPPING IN GRATITUDE

As a Christian EFT practitioner, I advocate only **ONE** exception to regularly tapping negatively: when saying prayers of thanksgiving. We have countless blessings to be thankful for, including our problems. One reason God allows us to have problems is to give us opportunities to grow and mature in Him as we trust He is working everything together for our good (Romans 8:28). Therefore, we give thanks in all things and for all things (1 Thessalonians 5:18; Ephesians 5:20).

Think about it: what happens when your children, grandbabies, nieces or nephews say, "Thank you"? You want to give them more! The same thing happens with God. When we demonstrate our trust in Him and are thankful, even in the hard times, He pours out His goodness and grace upon us. Our gratitude is like a magnet that pulls these blessings toward us.

By being thankful, you also "teach" your subconscious that life isn't as bad as it looks. Your negative beliefs are simply perceptions. I won't pretend that someone hasn't ever done something nasty to us in life, and that we most likely took away a negative message from the experience. Often, what was done to us wasn't meant in the way that our minds perceived it to be.

So much of how we think and feel about the world started decades ago when we were young and impressionable. As Apostle Paul says, it is time to stop thinking like a child, and begin thinking as an adult (1 Corinthians 13:11). Adult thinking is when God can use you for His purposes in His Kingdom; children aren't all that helpful in doing adult things!

Being thankful will change your entire outlook on life. A truly positive outlook on life helps keep our genetic markers in check, protecting us from sickness and disease.[107] According to the science of epigenetics, we up-regulate and down-regulate (turn and off) the expression of our genes. Remember: God instructs us in His

---

107 Church, *The Genie in Your Genes*, 163–164.

Word to be grateful. Physiologically, it's a great rule to follow, sowing our obedience and faith in Him, and often reaping the benefits of good health (Galatians 6:7–9).

To help you tap positive in Thanksgiving, I've included the following Scriptures. You can also launch into you are own reasons you are grateful—from hot water to refreshing rain to sweet peaches to whatever God has given you!

1 Thessalonians 5:18 – Give thanks in all circumstances; for this is the will of God in Christ Jesus for you.

Ephesians 5:20 – Giving thanks always and for everything to God the Father in the name of our Lord Jesus Christ.

Colossians 3:15–17 – And let the peace of Christ rule in your hearts, to which indeed you were called in one body. And be thankful. Let the word of Christ dwell in you richly, teaching and admonishing one another in all wisdom, singing psalms and hymns and spiritual songs, with thankfulness in your hearts to God. And whatever you do, in word or deed, do everything in the name of the Lord Jesus, giving thanks to God the Father through him.

Philippians 4:6 – Do not be anxious about anything, but in everything by prayer and supplication with thanksgiving let your requests be made known to God.

James 1:17 – Every good gift and every perfect gift is from above, coming down from the Father of lights with whom there is no variation or shadow due to change.

Colossians 4:2 – Continue steadfastly in prayer, being watchful in it with thanksgiving.

Colossians 3:17 – And whatever you do, in word or deed, do everything in the name of the Lord Jesus, giving thanks to God the Father through him.

Psalm 100:4 – Enter his gates with thanksgiving, and his courts with praise! Give thanks to him; bless his name!

Psalm 95:2 – Let us come into his presence with thanksgiving; let us make a joyful noise to him with songs of praise!

1 Chronicles 29:13 – And now we thank you, our God, and praise your glorious name.

Isaiah 12: 4–5 – And you will say in that day: "Give thanks to the Lord, call upon his name, make known his deeds among the peoples, proclaim that his name is exalted. "Sing praises to the Lord, for he has done gloriously; let this be made known in all the earth.

Psalm 30:12 – That my glory may sing your praise and not be silent. O Lord my God, I will give thanks to you forever!

Our ultimate goal in Christian life is to surrender to God, allowing Him to guide and facilitate every facet of our life on earth. Our desire is to do life together with Him—here and now, sharing His thoughts, feeling His heart and enjoying sweet fellowship. Intimacy with God is what we were created for. Communion is the desire of His heart!

CHAPTER 18

Make Room in Your Heart
by Charity Kayembe

While talking with Sherrie one day about tapping, I realized I didn't understand how tapping positive could be a negative experience. I tapped positive often, and I loved it! Why so negative, and why devote an entire chapter to its benefits? As I prayed into this, the Lord orchestrated two experiences: one in waking life, the second in a dream. They both illustrated how He designed negative and positive tapping to work. And, of course, Sherrie was right!

Although I tap positive and tap negative, I finally became aware that I rarely do both together at the same time. I don't have specific daily sessions; I simply tap on anything I'm feeling throughout the day. When I wake up, I tap while I meditate on the dream God gave me that previous night, as it prolongs my time in the quiet alpha brainwave state, keeping me connected to my heart.

When I read and ponder Scripture, I often tap. This again connects me quickly and easily with my spirit and Holy Spirit who is joined to my spirit (1 Corinthians 6:17). I receive His revelation and insights much more easily because I have purposefully positioned myself to connect with His river within me through Emotional Freedom Techniques.

The problem lies here: trying to tap positive when I feel negative. In my "how it works" example of the rude phone caller in Chapter Eleven, I tapped negative to get over my offense. Had I tried to be positive in the middle of my tapping rant by inserting Scripture, I would have failed miserably. Although all Scripture is true, not one was my truth at that moment. None would have stuck because it wouldn't have gone deep.

WHAT *NOT* TO DO

I learned the hard way why it's not good to tap positive too soon when I tried the method with a friend. Being a strong Christian, my friend understandably wanted to tap on only one or two brief negative statements about his current situation before immediately going into positive tapping and piling on Scripture.

I love Scripture. The Bible is my favorite Book. But more than simply quoting Scripture, I want to experience it. I want to feel its living and active truth flowing in and through me.

When my friend told me his situation, I suggested we tap. He quickly tapped positive, but it didn't help anything. Granted, we tapped for 2 minutes only, and in that time a creative solution did bubble up to the surface, which he hadn't before considered—a God thought that infused Christ's light and hope in an otherwise dark place. And for that, we were grateful! However, I wanted more.

I wanted a huge breakthrough and freedom for my friend, and we didn't get there because we didn't stay negative long enough to get to the root issue. I felt bad about our results and guilty that I hadn't explained the process better and helped my friend more.

Of course, I tapped on those negative feelings. That's when I finally received God's understanding of how the technique works. He explained *when* to move into effective positive tapping: only after the *Logos* has become *rhema*. I'll explain.

THE WORD FOR 'WORD'

Logos is Greek for "word" and is often used to refer to the written Word of God, the Bible. *Rhema* is also Greek for "word"; however, it refers to the spoken word. So we read the *Logos* and we pray for Holy Spirit to breathe on it and inspire it and apply it personally to our lives as revelatory *rhema*—turning God's written Word into spoken word.

> **Examples of God's written Word *(Logos)*:**
>
> "I have loved you with an everlasting love" (Jeremiah 31:3).
>
> You are "predestined for adoption according to God's good pleasure" (Ephesians 1:5).

Example of spoken word *(rhema):*

"Charity, I have loved you from before the beginning until after the end, and every moment in between. It's awesome being your Dad and I'm crazy about you, girl!"

The different examples are the same truth, but *rhema* is real-time and in the first-person. It is Spirit-breathed inspiration whispered into my heart by God Himself. It's for me, for now. This fits into the tapping narrative in an important way.

HOW FEELINGS TRUMP THOUGHTS

Next, I'll address the guilt I experienced for not helping my friend tap more effectively. Immediately, as I started tapping about how bad I felt, my *mind* said, "Don't worry, God causes all things to work together for good."

Well, that's true. He does. But at that moment, it was the written Word of God *(Logos)*. It was biblical truth, but it wasn't my truth. I sure didn't feel our session had worked out well, so trying to tap in Scripture would have also failed. Feelings are the filter that allow energy to move in and out of my subconscious spirit and cells.

Even though my head thought of a verse, I ignored it and continued tapping negatively. *Because when we are upset, we can only tap in the spoken word* (rhemas), *not the written Word of God* (Logos). We must wait for the *rhema* to flow from our hearts. Slapping a memorized verse of *Logos* on the problem won't stick. However, once the *rhema* word bubbles up, it will feel true to us. Since it feels true, we can tap it in. We only tap what feels true because emotion is the energy that activates and releases the spirit.

Because I still felt bad, I could only honestly and with sincerity tap negatively. That was what felt true to me in that moment: "I can't believe I couldn't help my friend. I should have said something differently! I feel so guilty I got his hopes up. What an epic failure. This is all my fault!"

TAPPING IN THE RHEMAS

I continued tapping negatively until I had a positive thought from someplace else. It was not from my mind; it was from my heart. And it bubbled up from deep within, up to the surface, as I was tapping.

The thought "just came to me" spontaneously: "You know, it's really awesome timing for you to have this bad experience with tapping positively. It's *kairos* (right opportune moment). You were just suggesting to Sherrie you weren't sure about focusing so much attention on negative tapping in your upcoming book. You suggested that chapter should, perhaps, be adjusted or softened. No way! It's *good* that this happened right now. *This* is how I'm causing all things to work together for good."

Those final words are the exact words from Romans 8:28, which my mind thought earlier. The difference was they were now Spirit-breathed and personally applied to my life and current situation—for me, for now. They felt true. And when Scripture feels true, then we know it's time to tap it in.

OUT OF OUR INNERMOST BEING

From where did that spontaneous thought and revelation originate? My heart— where Holy Spirit and His river of living water flow from. The scriptural truth bubbled up and it felt right. The Hebrew for prophecy is *naba*, which means to "bubble up." The *Logos* had become *rhema*, personalized and specific from God to me in this moment. It was then that I knew I could effectively and effectually tap it in.

In their book, *4 Keys to Hearing God's Voice*[108], my parents Mark and Patti Virkler teach that hearing the Lord's voice is as simple as quieting yourself down, looking for vision, tuning to spontaneity, and writing.

These keys are similar to what we do in EFT, and they achieve similar results. Through tapping we calm ourselves down and tune to our spontaneous inner flow. And in both cases, we are connecting to the river of God within us.

We see this phenomenon often with tapping. The prophetic *rhema* words from God—words of wisdom and words of knowledge—that aren't consciously known in our mind, flow effortlessly and spontaneously to the surface as we tap. We are connecting to the river of the Holy Spirit within us when we practice EFT. It is His flow of living water welling from our innermost being and bubbling up to the surface (John 7:37–39).

---

108 Virkler, *4 Keys to Hearing God's Voice*, 2010.

WHAT "BUBBLING UP" LOOKS LIKE IN EFT

I tapped with a pastor who was a counselor and who had also received a great deal of counseling herself. She never understood why she struggled so much with her weight. After a few minutes of tapping, it "came up" that her weight gain started when she was a child, the year her parents divorced.

She had tried to control her parents' relationship and help fix it, but she couldn't. She then began gaining weight—a cushion to separate and insulate herself from her situation. She finally realized the connection between helplessly trying to control her eating and fixing her weight and the inability to control her parents' relationship.

She was amazed how the underlying root issue just "came to her" when years of talk therapy had failed to reveal it. This can be likened to Isaac taking the Philistine's earth out of the wells (Genesis 26:15). The rivers of living water are deep in the innermost being, and tapping lets them bubble up to the surface.

Here again, we see how we are able to tap into the flow of divine thoughts and wisdom within. We are tapping into God's supernatural feelings and holy emotions. We're tapping into the Kingdom of God, and the very heart of the King Himself. Whoever is united with the Lord is one spirit with Him (1 Corinthians 6:17). We want to do everything we can to live out of that heart union with God, and tapping can be an effective tool to do precisely that.

I HAD A DREAM

I had discussed with Sherrie my initial confusion on when we should tap positive, and afterwards I meditated on the issue. The Lord then graciously shared more of His perspective with me through a dream, which confirmed what He had begun teaching me in waking life. He often reveals spiritual truths through my visions of the night, and this was no exception.

My dream showed various scenes. The one that impacted me most as I awoke was a bathroom scene. I jotted down details immediately and then meditated with Holy Spirit on what He was showing me through these dream sequences.

To understand the symbolism from my interpretation, you need some background from my waking life. Years ago, my family was doing ministry in Singapore. On a day off, our hosts invited us to a very swanky, high-end mall, filled with well-heeled shoppers wearing some of the most expensive designer clothes and handbags.

One of the restrooms in this ritzy mall was a bit of a surprise to my American mindset. When I entered, I saw the typical western commodes. In addition, I saw *very posh* squatty-pottys. I had never seen such classy-looking, sparkling porcelain squatty-pottys anywhere before!

That night after talking with Sherrie, I had a dream of a beautifully shining eastern-style commode in all its gleam and glory, just as I'd seen in Asia. That was the most striking symbol.

In the dream, I was visiting with friends. I wanted to change my sweater, so I went into their hallway bathroom. It was a very tiny room, and the entire floor was overtaken by this large and lovely squatty-potty. The space, therefore, was very cramped. This made balancing around the potty quite difficult. All I wanted to do in the bathroom was to put on a different sweater. But that wasn't the biggest problem.

My friend had all her jewelry hanging on little hooks in this bathroom. Stunning necklaces, bracelets and rings hung ever so precariously right above the big toilet basin. I thought, *Good grief! She should totally have her jewelry in another room in the house. This isn't good to have everything in the same space like this. She really should move these beautiful items to another room, as this just isn't the place to keep them!*

God's message to me through that dream was clear. He got me on the same page with how He was feeling. The dream was about my struggle to "change" (sweaters), and change is what we attempt to accomplish through EFT—change our thoughts, feelings and behaviors and "clothe ourselves with Christ" (Romans 13:14). The dream showed that there are times and places for some things to be done, and different, separate places for other things to be done. Both are important, but they are to remain separate.

KITCHENS AND BATHROOMS

The other thought Holy Spirit gave me upon awakening was that tapping in Scripture and positive truth is nourishment. It's like feeding our spirits and cells, strengthening and fortifying them. Eating the Word of God is akin to eating in the kitchen—a specific room designated for meals—the place we eat.

It also occurred to me what you do in kitchens should be done in the kitchen only, not the bathroom. And vice versa since, we don't eat food in the bathroom. We have two different places for two different purposes.

It's no different with our hearts. One room in our heart is where we are peaceful, grateful and tapping in Scriptural promises and beautiful visions from the Lord. Emotionally and spiritually, we are in a specific space in our hearts.

Another room in our heart is where we go when we've had an argument with a relative, an unfriendly exchange on the phone, we're stressed about work or whatever other negative situation we are experiencing. This is a different space in our hearts.

We are in a different room and place, and never the twain shall meet. In the bathroom, we rid ourselves of unnecessary waste. We also cleanse ourselves in the shower. This is where we tap negative.

After we are completely finished with our bathroom rituals, we walk down the hall and enter the "kitchen of our hearts," where we feed ourselves with the truth of God's Word. This is where we tap positive.

Our hearts, like our homes, provide two different spaces for two different purposes. This is what the dream showed: we need various and separate rooms. The bathroom is important as is the kitchen! But let's keep what belongs in each area in that area, and not confuse the two.

Therefore, should we tap negatively only? Yes. Should we tap positively only? Yes. We simply need to be aware of which room in our heart we happen to be in.

SUB-SECTION FIVE:
Good News!

CHAPTER 19

Surrender, Evangelism and EFT

"Surrender" is a warfare term, and it often implies "weakness or the inability to protect oneself." "Unconditional surrender" means "all rights and privileges are given to the victor." Surrendering to God works in much the same way. We set aside our own selfish agendas and eagerly seek His purpose for our lives. The wonderful news is God's plans for us are always in our best interest (Jeremiah 29:11) whereas our own plans often lead to our destruction (Proverbs 14:12). Our Lord's intentions for us are far better than any ideas we could ever dream up ourselves! He is able to do immeasurably more than all we ask or imagine, according to his power that is at work within us (Ephesians 3:20).

Our heart is the area of our conscience and the seat of our emotions, our values, and the place from where we make our decisions for God (Proverbs 4:23; Matthew 12:34–35). Scripture mentions a great deal about heart-centered living. Today much research[109] supports the concept that our "energy" resides in our heart. Even HeartMath Institute, a leading researcher in the area of heart and emotional science, conducted a study that showed our heart has an electromagnetic field 5000 times stronger than our brain's.[110]

HeartMath offers a free e-book titled *Science of the Heart, Exploring the Role of the Heart in Human Performance*.[111]

Many religions require its participants to adhere to strict codes of dress, acts, creeds, and systems of behavior. Our God wants our hearts and minds. He re-

---

109 www.heartmath.org/resources/infographic/mysteries-of-the-heart/
110 Kelly, *The Human Antenna*, 121–122; Church, *The Genie in Your Genes*, 118.
111 You may download *Science of the Heart* at www.heartmath.org/research/science-of-the-heart/

quests we be fully devoted to Him personally, not to the earthly ideas of religion. Christianity, too, has a biblical basis for its moral code, but our desires to follow those rules are second to our devotion to God. Adherence to these rules is the result of our love for our God, Who saved us when He sent Jesus to Calvary to atone for our sins. "We love because He first loved us" (1 John 4:19).

Our unconditional surrender to God is an ongoing process in which we choose to apply His omniscient viewpoint to our lives—minute by minute, day in and day out. We desire to see life and all His children through His divine perspective, not our human myopia. Emotional Freedom Techniques can facilitate this surrendering of our life more fully to God and to His "perceptions," which is Truth itself.

When Christian clients ask me how EFT might benefit them, I impart that EFT can bring them closer than ever to our Savior. Naturally, most are curious as to exactly how that happens.

As I explain that EFT can remove the hidden barriers that keep us from seeing and *feeling* God, and Who He really is, my clients begin to get excited. Most exclaim declarations like, "That's exactly what I'm looking for!"

When we lead lives that are sinful, half-hearted, and filled with emotional and physical pain, we are often so preoccupied with our own adversity that God is the last thing on our minds—except, of course, when we cry out to Him for help. A cry that often makes us sound more like a whiney child than a grateful believer. I know my cries surely did!

EFT removes barriers to God through our same fearfully and wonderfully made physiology that traps us. God created mankind perfectly, but Adam and Eve ruined that perfection in the Garden of Eden. Genesis 3:19 states, "By the sweat of your brow you will eat your food until you return to the ground, since from it you were taken; for dust you are and to dust you will return."

Adam and Eve went from a wonderful world of abundant provision to a life in which every morsel of food had to be gathered from the earth by their own hard work. When sin entered the world through our first parents' disobedience, our personal emotions took a turn for the worse. The Bible doesn't speak to this directly, but Adam and Eve surely felt anger, regret, remorse, resentment, and dozens of other emotions when God banned them from the Garden forever. These emotions must have also created a negative tangle of physiological responses. The shock and questioning of what had just happened must have been overwhelming and near unbearable.

Because of that event we, too, now have that jumble of mixed emotions and physical responses coursing through our bodies. We experience every human emotion as Adam and Eve felt—some good, some bad.

Sometimes, I picture Adam and Eve slumped over, walking down a treeless, hardened dirt road, dejected, as the door to Eden slams shut loudly behind them! They must have truly felt sorry for themselves!

Whether we sin or we suffer the result of someone else's sin foisted on us it often leaves us feeling sad and sorry for ourselves. Dejected, like Adam and Eve, we walk life's road muttering to ourselves, cursing the one who put us in this rotten position, clouding our vision of where to go or how to get ourselves out of the mess we find ourselves in.

Our God-created physiology immediately records and encodes of all of these feelings. Once these hurt emotions are locked in place, we build on them like a block wall of an unfinished basement. Stone by stone, our wall rises—thicker, higher, and more confining—until we have blocked ourselves into a very small space. Most often we don't see the build up, nor do we understand how it even happened since it often begins very early in childhood.

By the time we are adults, the wall is in place, strong and sturdy, a fortress that protects us from all incoming emotional hurts; our subconscious does the job God created for it to do.

Our fully formed, fully human mind perceives only the pallet of pain, nothing else. And so we complain, gripe, and whine about life, as if nothing is to be done about it. Now, today, we know better! We often can do something about it with EFT.

DOING THE WORK

As I personally tap with people from all walks of life nationwide, I often hear the whoops and a holler of, "Hallelujah," for what God does in their lives. The caveat is these clients understand the power of God as they tap. And they understand that in order to really receive the full effect of tapping, they must tap daily. They have taken my admonition to heart: "You get out of tapping exactly what you put into it."

In other words, five minutes of tapping yields five minutes of results. If we want something to work well in life, we must invest the time and effort to learn it well and practice it. The same rule applies with EFT. Tapping is a lifestyle change. **Rule 1:** you must purpose in your heart to tap regularly and seek the Holy Spirit's equipping grace to empower you to accomplish this goal.

Rule 2: tapping has to be effectively engaged. Meaning, you should go deeply enough to allow God to heal you. Most often, you can't achieve this by yourself. It is nearly impossible for us alone to approach the emotional pain we have all done our best to avoid our entire lives!

If someone has deep-seated, painful life events, they must hire an experienced EFT practitioner to tap with them. It is a necessity. While it is true that EFT is a self-help tool, the self-help part begins once the big, the bad, and the ugly events and memories are dealt with through the help of an experienced coach who has traveled that path before you.

What you can reap through tapping well and neutralizing many of the major negative memories in your life is multi-fold. Tapping is God's gift for releasing those leftover emotions. Literally, it's like cutting satan off at the knees. EFT can eliminate his effectiveness to lead us into sin. As our negative emotions fade away, so often does our resistance to hear the Lord and follow His lead. This results in the biggest and best gift of EFT: complete and unconditional surrender to God Himself. Our thoughts align with the mind of Christ. Our emotions align with the fruit of His Spirit. We come into full agreement with our Father and His heart.

Many of the people with whom I tap surrendered their lives to Jesus Christ decades ago. They may rededicate their lives a time or two over the years, hoping to get back on track in their Christian journeys. But still, they find themselves stuck in the same old sinkholes and bad habits.

This is where the beauty of God's EFT comes in! Continuing to be stuck in sinkholes and bad habits is the leftover residue of our sin nature. We tend to carry around condemnation for past sins. Condemnation is not from God; that is the enemy harassing us.

Think about it this way: When your 3-year-old—son, grandson, niece or nephew—is engrossed in playing with his Legos, and you ask him to put his toys away, what happens? Right. Nothing! The child's mind is so preoccupied with building his castle, he doesn't even hear you, let alone comply.

Many of us are emotional 3-year-olds. Life's bound us so tightly in its trials and travails, we barely hear God speaking to us! We live life reacting to one event after another. We do no planning or proactive thinking; it's all go, go, go—react, react, react.

EFT can interrupt this chain reaction. Most of the non-stop action in your life is a response to the events of your past. You are on automatic pilot. You've done something a certain way for as long as you can remember that these old habits tell you to stay the course. That course isn't always the most healthy or in your best interest, but still you repeat the action. You have no time to think, and most definitely you have no time to pray or read Scriptures.

God can use EFT to re-prioritize your life. He can use tapping to stop you in your subconscious tracks, so you become conscious of thought processes you may never have analyzed or considered before. Under the illumination of the Holy Spirit, God fills in the missing pieces, pointing out to you why you do the things you do, and perhaps He will show you a better way to live.

MARY'S BIRTHDAY PARTY

While tapping with a client I'll name Mary, she began recalling her anger at her father. He was always very disapproving of anything she ever did. The event she remembered was a birthday party she had at seven years old.

Mary pictured in her mind the birthday party her Mom had put together for her. Six of her school friends attended. During the party, one of the girls asked Mary to pass the pitcher of milk to her. As Mary did so, she ran her elbow into the icing of her chocolate cake.

Her father, standing next to her, saw her elbow hit the cake, and he quickly pushed her elbow away. In so doing, it knocked the entire cake onto the kitchen floor. All the girls began to laugh enthusiastically. Mary was instantly mortified. As she turned bright red with embarrassment, her father barked, "Why are you always so stupid? Don't you know better than to reach over an iced cake?"

While tapping now, a light bulb switched on and Mary understood consciously for the first time why she detested crowds and gatherings that involved any smid-gen of a party atmosphere. This fear was problematic in her life because her job required hosting in-office entertaining for high-level executives when they came to town.

Every time her boss asked her to set-up for such a "party" affair, Mary's anxiety and insecurity rose to near panic level. She could never figure out the why of her reactions since it didn't really seem like such a big deal on the surface.

After tapping and neutralizing her father's comments around that early in life birthday party, Mary never again had any angst when her boss asked her to prepare to entertain out of town guests.

Multiply this simple example by 100, and you start to get some idea of how God may be able to transform your life through tapping! What happens to you if you have past negative memories of a sexual event, a terrible crime you witnessed, or a parent who drank ceaselessly, creating a scene every time you had a friend come to the house?

Those memories often set you up for a life you don't want or understand. And as much as you surrender the pain and present the events to your Savior, nothing ever seems to change for the better. The surrender and peace that can often come from releasing our painful past through EFT is beyond words! It is so sweet, so tender that it nearly melts your heart.

EFT for Christians gives you the opportunity to live in child-like wonder as you allow Jesus to hold you in His arms. Luke 18:13 reads, "Truly I tell you, unless you change and become like little children, you will never enter the kingdom of heaven."

I have pondered that verse since starting all of my own tapping. Often, EFT really can bring you into surrender-like mode when tapping is done well and completely. In other words, you should keep tapping until the core issues are resolved.

As we tap away all the worry about the future that is perpetuated by events of the past in our subconscious mind, that surrender seems to become easier and easier. God lifts the heaviness off our chests, allowing us to trust Him more and more in our daily lives. Proverbs 3:5–6 becomes more a reality by the day: "Trust in the LORD with all your heart and lean not on your own understanding; in all your ways submit to him, and he will make your paths straight." Amen!

Surrendering to God and tapping seem to go hand in hand. There appears to be a beautiful symbiotic relationship between the two. The more we surrender to tapping, the more surrendered to God we seem to become. The more we tap, the less we worry about the future, which is even deeper surrender to God's will. It appears the more we surrender, the more God shows us what else to tap on to clear our life for more surrender to Him. Once this new habit, thought process, and healing are in place, it looks to become a *good* cycle. You can change your synaptic neural connections to move in a positive manner toward Jesus.

As we calm our minds through tapping, we move into the slower meditative alpha and theta brainwave states, thus enabling us to hear the Holy Spirit more clearly. As the clutter of our mind clears, God's still, small voice can be better heard. He need not navigate through all the noise to be heard!

It appears to be a wonderful new cycle, replacing the old thought patterns of fear and stress in our subconscious, which opposes God's thoughts of peace and purpose (Isaiah 26:3).

> The sweet surrender can offer a new life path that is exemplified in Romans 12:2, *"Do not conform to the pattern of this world, but be transformed by the renewing of your mind. Then you will be able to test and approve what God's will is—his good, pleasing and perfect will."*

TAKING OTHERS WITH US

Our job here on earth is to glorify our Father in heaven. If we know our lives aren't glowing with God works—for us and in us—then we need to find a better way to remove the barriers that stop us from showing others Christ in us. EFT seems to be that better way.

But the benefits can go even further! As we use EFT to eliminate our emotional trauma and negative memories, we are most often drawn to the throne of God. God uses EFT to part the "Red Sea waters" of our mind. He seems to clear the cloudiness of our unbelief or resistance for us to give every area of our life to Christ.

In other words, EFT can be an evangelism tool for the Church. As others watch the emotional and physical lives of Christians heal, they will want part of that action!

"Evangelism" means "good news" and is derived from the Greek *euaggelion*, which means "gospel." The verb form of *euaggelizesthai*, which means "to bring," occurs fifty-five times in the New Testament, and is normally translated as "preach" (e.g., Acts 8:4, Acts 8:25, Acts 8:35, Acts 11:20).

Preaching the good news is exactly what we do when we tell others how well EFT seems to work – we preach the news of healing! We extol what God has done in our lives, for us, through His powerful healing.

What better way to introduce non-believers to Christ than to help them tap. As they feel their emotional pains melt away, you then have an opportunity to introduce them to the God Who just healed them. A God Who cares deeply for all of our needs. One Who wants us whole and healthy and blessed.

EFT is a powerful evangelism tool, and the following story is a great illustration:

This is another case study written by Dee Whitaker LeGrand using her own words:

FROM LIMITING BELIEF TO BELIEF IN GOD

Tim's life had been full of hardships, and it had gotten the better of him time and time again. A childhood robbed of love, security, and confidence led by an emotionally distant father and a very anxious mother created a residual anxiety of never being enough, having enough, or feeling safe.

This set off a chain of unhealthy emotional events that, at age 50, he still had not managed to control, no matter how hard he tried. Every time he thought he had a handle on his emotions, unexpected turns made him question everything, including himself.

He started off our first session by telling me about his issue of not feeling good enough to handle money and the pain in his lower back. It seemed he never had enough money to take care of his family, had financial mishaps in the past, and was worried about the debt that continued to mount. As we talked, he uncovered deeply seated feelings that he didn't deserve good things, life was hard, and he would never get ahead.

I asked him about his lower back pain, and after some thought, he said his lower back pain flared when he felt really stressed out. He had always taken an over-the-counter pain reliever to help keep it in check. However, it kept getting worse, even though his doctor could not find any physical reason for it.

He told me that when that voice "that comes from nowhere" speaks up, his back pain flares. I asked him to think back and tell me when that critical voice started, and if he recognized that voice. He remembered his parents arguing often about money. Mom would complain she didn't have enough to pay the bills or put groceries on the table. Dad would reply in a defensive tone that he was working as hard as he could. From the financial stress on the marriage, his father left the family and divorced his mother. He knew it was the combination of both parents that he heard in his head and still believed.

That was exactly what was happening in his life. As a child, he heard many times how his family did not have enough money to make ends meet, and it had become a self-fulfilling prophecy in his life with his own family. His wife would moan about their finances, their mounting debt, and his financial failures. He would then, in turn, become defensive and respond that he was doing the best he could. But secretly he felt deep in his soul he was a failure, and he would never make enough money to help his family get out of debt.

Feeling like a failure and not good enough are two of the deepest, most fundamental fears we can experience. We started his session by tapping on his childhood memories and childhood messages:

*Life was hard and I can't get ahead
I never have enough money and never will
When I think about success, it is for other people, but not for me
I grew up poor, so people like me can't find success
If I haven't been successful by now, chances are I never will*

Once those emotional triggers were cleared, he then wanted to work on his relationship with his wife and kids. He loved his wife as much as he knew how, but he seemed to be disconnected from his deep feelings. He felt she did not really understand him, his emotions and that he never felt supported. He also felt that disconnect with his children.

We once again went back to his childhood and tapped on:

My parents never had time for me
The scary feeling inside my body of not being safe
Not ever feeling truly loved

During our next session, he told me how much better his back felt. Emotion-
ally, he realized he was blocking his ability to love himself, therefore, blocking
his ability to feel love from his family. Up until this time, we had been using
phrases like, "Even though I have this problem, and feel _____, I am open
to the possibility/ it would be nice if I was able to accept myself."

We then used these phrases for the psychological reversal on the karate chop:

"Even though I don't feel like anyone loves me or has by back, I am open to
feeling and seeing this differently."

"Even though I have blocked love and feeling safe, I am open to deeply and
completely loving and accepting myself, and feeling safe."

"Even though I don't feel the love of my family, I am doing my best to heal and
in the process of loving and accepting myself."

"Even though I don't feel the depth of love that I need, I acknowledge feeling
this way. I am open to learning new ways of letting go of my past wounds, and
open myself up to the love my family has for me."

We tapped on his specific feelings and thoughts as he released his inner child-
hood emotional wounds. Over time, Tim came to see his life in a different
way. His perspective had changed about not being good enough or deserving
good things in his life. He looked at money in a different way and was more
confident to find another job that took care of his family's financial needs.

RE-RIGHT YOUR HISTORY WITH GOD

When we approached the subject of being safe, we took a different route. I
incorporated tapping with another method I use – "Re-right your history with
God."

In every session, I had been praying with him and talking to him about the
way he might see similarities between his earthly father and his Heavenly

Father. We talked about the limiting beliefs of not feeling dad was there for him or never having time for him, which made him feel dad never loved him or had his back.

He replied that even though he had learned about God as a child in church, and remembered bits and pieces of sermons of God's love for us, and that He sent His Son to the cross for us. He always thought that yes, he could envision God doing that for others, but he was not sure that meant him. He still had reservations about opening his heart.

I asked him if he wanted to try an additional method along with tapping—an approach that would take him back to when he first thought of God not being there for him and loving him the way God loved others. He still seemed hesitant, so we tapped on:

"Even though I don't feel safe enough yet to let the walls to my heart down to trust God, I accept my feelings, and I love and accept myself, and I am open to the possibility that God might love and accept me just as I am."

We tapped variations of the set up statement 5 times, and then specific tapping with 6 rounds of tapping on his uncertainty until his intensity or SUDS level was at a 3.

I then asked him to go back in his memory and find the first time he remembered God not coming through for him.

THE DIVORCE

He was 8 years old, and his dad had just told him he was leaving because he and his mom couldn't get along. Tim begged him to stay and work things out, telling him how much he needed him, but his dad said he had made up his mind and was getting a divorce.

After his dad left, he remembered going to his parents' bedroom and grabbing his dad's pillow. He took it to his room and cried into it for hours. I gently led Tim back to his 8-year-old younger self so that part of him could be comforted. He remembered and saw younger Tim on his bed still crying.

As we tapped, I prayed over him, inviting God to make His Father's heart known to Tim. I instructed Tim to keep tapping and become aware of any stirrings in his heart. He was repeating the words he remembered while his younger self cried out to his father not to leave him. He needed his dad and wanted to know what it felt like to feel his love. As he continued to tap, I continued to pray softly for God to make Himself known to Tim. His heart was open and ready.

THE BREAKTHROUGH

After a while, Tim stopped tapping, lifted up his head, and looked at me. His eyes were dry and inquisitive. I asked him what he was feeling, and all he could say was he was not familiar with these emotions and the warm feeling in his heart. As he explained to me, his heart was calm, and he was almost scared of this because he was afraid it would not last, and he would go back to the old way of feeling and thinking.

I gently led him back to the memory, so he could talk with younger Tim. I asked him to sit with him, console and tell the younger Tim he was there for him. After younger Tim calmed down, I asked Tim to tell his younger self there was someone who would give him the security he needed and would never leave him. It was time to introduce Tim to his Heavenly Father.

As we continued to tap, God made himself known to Tim. I saw it in his face and in his demeanor. He silently had a conversation with God, crying and laughing with tears streaming down his face. He then looked at me, and I asked him what he felt. "Peace," he replied. It was such a foreign feeling that he shook his head to try and figure out what was stirring in his heart.

We then tapped on welcoming God into his life.

During our next session, we tapped and talked about the different perspective he now had. He had found a church where the people welcomed him and made him feel at home. And there was also a new home in his heart, where he welcomed God.

One recent service, the pastor had an altar call and Tim knew he was ready to take the next step, the most vital step in his spiritual life, by receiving Jesus as his Lord and Savior. Tim walked forward to the altar to give his life to

Christ. This completed him. He found all that he was deprived of. For the first time in his life, he knew the safety, peace and abundance of God the Father and God the Son.

BLESSED AND LOVED

I still see Tim from time to time to work on spiritual or emotional issues that come up. He often tells me how much his life has changed. "I am a blessed and loved man," he boasts. I have everything I need now, after meeting and accepting Jesus through my Heavenly Father.

Dee Whitaker LeGrand is a Christian EFT Coach, Christian Life Coach, Emotional Wellness Coach and a Relationship Coach. She is passionate about working with her clients, as she helps them release their emotional wounds, trauma, negative thoughts and beliefs so God can heal their hearts and souls. This blessed work fulfills the purpose God has intended for her in this season of her life. Dee incorporates inner healing and deliverance, spiritual cleansing when needed within her EFT Coaching practice.[112]

God is indeed faithful. He can renew your mind, smooth out your path, shower you with His mercy and empower you to live in His grace. He will transform your will to His as you tap for Him.

If you would like to get closer to God we invite you to visit www.bornofthespirit. today. This website will answer your spiritual questions and shine the light of God's Word and His love upon you as you explore your own unfolding journey with Him. God is better than you think! And He can't wait to flood your heart with His compassion and your life with His goodness, presence, peace and joy. Every blessing to you!

---

112 Dee Whitaker can be reached for a free 15-minute consultation at www.ChristianEFT.Info

CHAPTER 20

Living to a Different Kingdom
by Charity Kayembe

"The Kingdom of God is within you." (Luke 17:21 KJV)

The word Kingdom means the domain of the King. It is where the King has dominion and where He rules. Although we absolutely want to experience the glory of His Kingdom manifest in our natural world, it must first manifest within us—in the hearts and minds of the children of the King.

WHERE IS THE KINGDOM?

The King must rule in the thoughts of our minds. The King must rule in the feelings of our hearts. How can we give away something we have yet to experience? How can we shine His light in the world if our minds are still dark, not enlightened with the light of life? How can we share His love and compassion with the world if we don't feel love and won't forgive ourselves?

Jesus said, "The Kingdom of God is within you" (Luke 17:21). He wants to extend His rule and to advance His Kingdom, and He says it starts with us. It starts *in* us. When our thoughts match His thoughts, and we live into the mind of Christ—that's the Kingdom of God (1 Corinthians 2:16). When our emotions match His emotions, and we live into the fruit of the Spirit—that's the Kingdom of God (Galatians 5:22).

The best way to experience His rule and reign in the world is to experience His rule and reign in our lives personally—moment by moment, our thoughts obeying Christ (2 Corinthians 10:5), and our feelings aligned with God's heart (1 Corinthians 13:13).

The Kingdom of Heaven isn't far removed from us, off in the distant future. The Kingdom begins inside of us. And it starts right now.

EFT: ENFORCING THE KING'S DOMAIN

So how can we get there? How can we live into and out of this Kingdom? As we have seen, this is where practicing Emotional Freedom Techniques comes into play. Tapping can empower us to release the fears and phobias, worry and anxiety, anger, stress and sadness that engulf us. We know these negative feelings have been subjected to the King's rule. These are not God's best for us, and now we can release the negativity and step into blessing. Now we are equipped to get from where we are to where we should be. How can we experience the abundant life for which Christ died? We tap into it!

We trust you've been encouraged and inspired throughout this book as you have discovered how EFT can connect you to the heavenly kingdom within. Tapping can get us in touch with our hearts, where Christ lives (Ephesians 3:17). In His presence is fullness of joy (Psalm 16:11). His love and peace overwhelm the dark spaces in our hearts and minds, flooding them with the light of His glory.

Ephesians 4:18 illustrates how our minds can be darkened, and 2 Corinthians 4:6 reveals God's desire of His light to shine in our hearts. We don't have to struggle and fight the dark thoughts and emotions. We simply have to live in the light. Tapping can connect us to the Light of the World, who lives within us (John 8:12). Indeed, we were formerly darkness, but now we ourselves are light in the Lord (Ephesians 5:8). EFT can keep us plugged in to His infinite power source.

This is an overdue conversation that must be had. Jesus died for us to live in His peace and joy and hope and love today—not in the sweet by and by. Tapping can be a vehicle that moves us into that safe, positive place—here and now. We don't have to wait any longer; Jesus already gave us all His blessing, healing, provision and salvation at the cross. We must actively receive and appropriate these gifts and live as if our prayers have already been answered because, in fact, they already have (1 John 5:14–15).

LIVING FROM OUR HEART

When our mind is in the alpha brainwave state, the inner world is more real than the outer world. We are not looking at the things that are seen, but the things unseen (2 Corinthians 4:18). That's living to the Kingdom of Heaven within us.

Scientifically proven, EFT moves us into our alpha-level brainwave state, in which we are our most peaceful, intuitive and creative. Even if that were the only benefit, it would be reason enough to tap early and tap often! I go out of my way every single day to live in this alpha state. I undertake dream interpretation work because we receive dreams during alpha-state REM sleep. I pray and sing in tongues throughout the day because that shifts me from analytical beta brainwaves into the desired meditative and reflective alpha state.[113]

Dream work, praying in tongues, tapping—I often engage in all three activities simultaneously. I meditate on my night vision from heaven, pray into it in the Spirit, and tap the revelation deep into my cells and my heart. When we experience life while in the alpha brainwave state, we have moved down into our spirit and are living from our heart zone. Jesus lives in our hearts, so we want to live into our heart—and out of our heart as well. From our heart flows everything else in our lives (Proverbs 4:23).

The Lord spoke an awesome word to one of my graduate students, Patty Sadallah, in her journaling time. God confirmed His intimate connection with each one of us when He explained, *"If I held My breath, all creation would cease to exist."* Yes!

The Hebrew word for "breath" also means "spirit." In Genesis, we read that God breathed into man the breath of life, and he became a living being. It is the very Spirit and breath of God Himself that animates, energizes and gives life to our physical bodies.

One of my favorite tapping verses is in the Book of Job: "The Spirit of God has made me, and the breath of the Almighty gives me life" (Job 33:4). Everyone has this spirit in them. All who are alive—they are breathing God's breath. Christ is all and is in all (Colossians 3:11). Indeed, He is not far from any one of us, for it is in Him that we live and move and have our being (Acts 17:27–28).

---

113 Van der Kolk, *The Body Keeps the Score*, 320–322.

We want His Spirit to flow unhindered. We want His energy to surge through us unimpeded and unobstructed. We want His breath to move freely around us, within us, and through us. The spirit—or the literal translation *breath*—of man is the lamp of the Lord, searching the innermost parts of his being (Proverbs 20:27).

Through EFT we can remove barriers, allowing His Spirit to flow unrestrained. Through tapping we can unstop His River in our lives. This is one way to work out our soul's salvation, knowing it is God who is at work in us, accomplishing His good pleasure (Philippians 2:12–13). Dr. Mercola teaches that in EFT "the healing is not done by us, but through us."[114] Holy Spirit does the work. Holy Spirit is the one who heals us, gives us breakthrough and sets us free.

Through tapping, we simply position ourselves to allow His breath, river, spirit, energy, and presence to flow most powerfully through us. Can we stop the blessings of God? Of course we can. Can we position ourselves to receive the greatest outpouring available? Of course we can. The choice is ours. And EFT gives us a powerful way to choose well.

LIVING INTO HIS KINGDOM

We get to choose when we experience the Kingdom of Heaven. We can passively endure lives of quiet desperation, stressed out with worry, fear and addiction, but strangely comforted by the fact that at least when we die, it will get better. Once we have left this world, then we hope, at last, to know peace and experience joy in our eternal heavenly home.

Holy Spirit's revelation is for us to experience the atmosphere of Heaven today. We can live positive, know peace that passes understanding, and feel unspeakable joy here and now (1 Peter 1:8–9). We don't have to wait!

Jesus said the Kingdom of Heaven is at hand (Matthew 10:7). The Kingdom of Heaven has come near you (Luke 10:9). The Kingdom of Heaven is in your midst. The Kingdom of Heaven is within you (Luke 17:21). I'm not really sure how many other ways He can tell us, *"It's here! It's now! Live into Heaven and live out of it."*

As we discussed at the beginning of this book, the Kingdom of God is righteousness, peace and joy in the Holy Ghost (Romans 14:17). To the degree we are

---

114 Dr. Mercola's Emotional Freedom Techniques, Disc 1, Introduction

overwhelmed and not experiencing peace and rest, we are not living into His Kingdom. If we're allowing fear in our hearts, then we are not inside God's heart since He is love, and perfect love drives out fear (1 John 4:18). If we're not joyful, then we are not aware and living to the truth that He is with us since in His presence is fullness of joy (Psalm 16:11).

Checking our emotional state is a great way to gauge if we are living into the Kingdom the way Father desires. Are we experiencing His emotions of love, joy, peace and goodness—the fruit of His Spirit in our lives? If we are not feeling His feelings in any area of our life, we now know what to do. We can tap!

We no longer are environmentally dependent. We no longer look outside ourselves for happiness and contentment. It doesn't matter if we've had our cup of coffee yet or if it's raining outside. We are living to an inner Kingdom, and the Son is always shining there!

The atmosphere of Heaven is full of laughter; no one is scared or anxious. Everyone is peaceful and at rest. We can live into that Kingdom starting today, this very moment. Jesus said *on earth* as it is in Heaven (Matthew 6:10). He wants us to experience Heaven here, in this world, too!

WHAT GOD LOVES TO DO

As you come to the end of this book, I pray you receive the revelatory understanding all over again of just how much your heavenly Father loves you, and how it is His *good pleasure* to give you the Kingdom (Luke 12:32). He wants you living inside His place of peace and living inside His space of joy. He wants you living impervious to the elements of this natural world. You are no longer influenced by what your natural eyes see and physical ears hear. Now you are living to a different kingdom, one that is overflowing with laughter, faith, hope, and love.

You are equipped and invited to tap into God's holy emotions of peace and joy. Feel His forgiveness. Rejoice in His goodness. Know His grace. Experience His love.

Salvation is personal. Subjective. Emotional. God is love and Jesus is the Savior of the world, but until you make those absolute truths your own personal truth, they do nothing for you. They are of no benefit to your life (Romans 10:9–10).

Therefore, get personal between you and God. Intimately share your whole heart with Him—hold nothing back. All of Him loves all of you, and He can be trusted. Where the Spirit of the Lord is there is freedom, and now you know how to connect effectually and effortlessly with Him in your heart (2 Corinthians 3:17). You hold the key in your hands—in your very fingertips—to access Holy Spirit's healing power.

Live deeply from that sacred place. Tap into the compassionate heart of your heavenly Father. Tap into His presence and be anchored there. Tap into the super-natural reality of the Kingdom of God within. Live into the revelation. And live out of it. Christ in you—the hope of glory (Colossians 1:27). Amen!

ABOUT THE AUTHORS

SHERRIE RICE SMITH, R.N. (RETIRED)

Sherrie has more than four decades in nursing, which includes work in medical-surgical, home health, and hospice care. Sherrie has an intense interest in all things related to biology, physiology, psychology, and quantum mechanics. These interests allow for an understanding of the efficaciousness of Emotional Freedom Techniques. Her personal experience with EFT is based on her own life story, giving her an even greater appreciation of how well EFT can bring both physical and emotional healing when coupled with prayer and the knowledge that Jesus heals.

Sherrie holds two EFT certifications, mentors Christian EFT Practitioners and students, and teaches certification classes, levels 1 and 2, for EFTUniverse. She is also the author of *EFT for Christians*, originally published in 2015.

Sherrie and her husband, Brad, reside in Milwaukee and travel extensively throughout the United States. Please join Sherrie on Facebook at www.facebook.com/groups/352652964926202/ or www.facebook.com/groups/307887129394873/ or subscribe to Sherrie's EFT for Christians blog at http://eftforchristian.blogspot.com/

DR. CHARITY KAYEMBE

Charity earned her Master of Divinity and Doctor of Biblical Studies through Christian Leadership University. She is ordained through CWG Leaders Network and has worked alongside her parents, Mark and Patti Virkler, in ministry for twenty years (www.CWGMinistries.org).

Charity is an online Professor of Graduate Studies at CLU, where hearing God's voice is at the center of every learning experience. She is passionate about bringing Heaven to earth through restoring the supernatural to believers' everyday lives. Charity is the co-author of *Hearing God Through Your Dreams – Understanding the Language God Speaks at Night*. Please visit her blog at www.GloryWaves.org.

Her international outreach has taken her to all corners of the globe, traveling to more than 50 nations on six continents. She and her husband live in upstate New York.

BIBLIOGRAPHY

Although I have read or consulted the books in this bibliography as reference material and for informational purposes only, I do not advocate all of the ideas, thoughts, or methods/processes promoted in them. These books should be read through the lens of God's Word, at your own discretion.

Allender, Dan B., M.D. *The Wounded Heart, Hope for Adult Victims of Childhood Sexual Abuse.* Navpress: Colorado Springs, CO, 1995.

Barlett, Richard, N.C., N.D. *The Physics of Miracles.* Atria Books: New York, 2009.

Barr, Stephen. *Modern Physics and Ancient Faith.* University of Notre Dame Press: Notre Dame, IN, 2003.

Bonhoeffer, Dietrich. *Life Together: The Classic Exploration of Christian in Community.* HarperOne: San Francisco, CA, 2009.

Carrington, Patricia. *Discover the Power of Meridian Tapping: A Revolutionary Method for Stress-Free Living.* Try It Productions: Brookfield, CT, 2008.

Carter, Rita, ed. *Mapping the Mind.* University of California Press: CA, 1999.

Cherry, Reginald. *Healing Prayer.* Thomas Nelson: Nashville, TN, 1999.

Childre, Doc and Howard Martin. *The HeartMathSolution.* HarperOne: San Francisco, CA, 1999.

Church, Dawson, Ph.D. *The Genie in Your Genes: Epigenetic Medicine and the New Biology of Intention.* Energy Psychology Press: Santa Rosa, CA, 2014.

Dispenza, Joe, D.C. *Evolve Your Brain: The Science of Changing Your Mind.* Health Communications, Inc.: Deerfield Beach, FL, 2007.

Dossey, Larry. *Reinventing Medicine Beyond Mind-Body to a New Era of Healing.* HarperOne: San Francisco, CA, 1999.

Ecker, Bruce, Ticic, Robin, and Laurel Hulley. *Unlocking the Emotional Brain: Eliminating Symptoms at Their Roots Using Memory Reconsolidation.* Routledge: New York, 2012.

Elwell, Walter A., ed. *Evangelical Dictionary of Biblical Theology (Baker Reference Library).* Baker Publishing Group: Ada, MI, 1996.

Gallo, Fred P., Ph.D. and Harry Vincenzi, Ed.D. *Energy Tapping.* New Harbinger Publications: Oakland, CA, 2008.

Gribben, John. *In Search of Schrodinger's Cat: Quantum Physics and Reality.* Bantam Books: New York, 1984.

Hegstrom, Paul. *Broken Children, Grown-Up Pain: Understanding the Effects of Your Wounded Past.* Beacon Hill Press: Kansas City, MO, 2006.

Hoekema, Anthony A. *Created in God's Image.* William Eerdmans Publishing Co.: Grand Rapids, MI, 1986.

Hunter, Joan. *Power to Heal Receiving God's Everyday Miracles.* Whitaker Books: New Kensington, PA, 2009.

Jeeves, Malcolm and R.J. Berry. *Science, Life, and Christian Belief.* Baker Books: Grand Rapids, MI, 1998.

Johnson, Bill. *Hosting the Presence: Unveiling Heaven's Agenda.* Destiny Image: Shippensburg, PA, 2012.

Karr-Morse, Robin, and Meredith S. Wiley. *Ghosts from the Nursery.* Atlantic Monthly Press: New York, 1997.

Kelly, Robin, Dr. *The Human Antenna: Reading the Language of the Universe in the Songs of Our Cells.* Energy Psychology Press: Santa Rosa, CA, 2009.

Klatz, Ronald and Robert Goldman. *Stopping the Clock: Longevity for the New Millennium.* Basic Health: North Bergen, NJ, 2002.

Koch, Carl and Joyce Heil. *Meditating on Our Body Created in God's Image.* St. Mary's Press: Winona, MN, 1991.

Leader, Darian. *The New Black Mourning, Melancholia, and Depression.* Graywolf Press: Minneapolis, MN, 2008.

Leaf, Caroline, Dr. *Switch On Your Brain: The Key to Peak Happiness, Thinking, and Health.* Baker Books: Michigan, 2013.

Leaf, Caroline, Dr. *Who Switched Off My Brain.* Switch on Your Brain USA: TX, 2008.

Levine, Peter A., PhD. *In An Unspoken Voice: How the Body Releases Trauma and Restores Goodness.* North Atlantic Books: Berkeley, CA, 2010.

Lipton, Bruce, H., PhD. *The Biology of Belief: Unleashing the Power of Consciousness, Matter & Miracles.* Mountain of Love / Elite Books: San Rafael, CA, 2005.

Lipton, Bruce, H., Ph.D. *The Biology of Belief: Unleashing the Power of Consciousness, Matter & Miracles.* Hay House: Carlsbad, CA, 2008.

Mate, Gabor, M.D. *When the Body Says NO: Exploring the Stress-Disease Connection.* John Wiley & Sons: Hoboken, NJ, 2003.

Permutter, David, M.D. and Alberto Villoldo, Ph.D. *Power Up Your Brain.* Hay House: Carlsbad, CA, 2011.

Randall, Lisa. *Warped Passages: Unraveling the Mysteries of the Universe's Hidden Dimensions.* Harper Perennial: New York, 2005.

Pert, Candace B., Ph.D. *Everything You Need to Know to Feel Go(o)d.* Hay House, Inc.: Carlsbad, CA, 2006.

Pert, Candace B., Ph.D. *Molecules of Emotion.* Scribner: New York, 1997.

Richards, James B., Dr. *How to Stop the Pain.* Whitaker House: New Kensington, PA, 2001.

Smith, Edward M. *Healing Life's Hurts Through Theophostic Prayer.* New Creation Publishing: Royal Oak, MI, 2005.

Sternberg, Esther M., M.D. *The Balance Within: The Science of Connecting Health and Emotions.* W.H. Freeman and Company: New York, 2001.

Thiessen, Sarah J. *Splankna: The Redemption of Energy Healing for the Kingdom of God.* CrossHouse Publishing: Rockwall, TX, 2011.

Van der Kolk, Bessel A. *The Body Keeps the Score.* Viking: New York, 2014.

Virkler, Mark, Dr. and Charity Kayembe, Ph.D. *Hearing God Through Your Dreams.* Destiny Image: Shippensburg, PA, 2016.

Virkler, Mark, Dr. and Patti Virkler. *4 Keys to Hearing God's Voice.* Destiny Image: Shippensburg, PA, 2010.

White, John. *Putting the Soul Back in Psychology.* InterVarsity Press: Downers Grove, IL, 1987.

ONLINE SOURCES

"Significant grey matter changes in a region of the orbitofrontal cortex in healthy participants predicts emotional dysregulation", Predrag Petrovic, Carl Johan Ekman, Johanna Klahr, Lars Tigerström, Göran Rydén, Anette G. M. Johansson, Carl Sellgren, Armita Golkar, Andreas Olsson, Arne Öhman, Martin Ingvar and Mikael Landén, *Social Cognitive and Affective Neuroscience*, online: 15 juni 2015, doi: 10.1093/scan/nsv072.

http://c.ymcdn.com/sites/www.energypsych.org/resource/resmgr/imported/NeurochemistryCounterConditioningLane.pdf

http://innersource.net/ep/images/stories/downloads/Acupoint_Stimulation_Research_Review.pdf

Manufactured by Amazon.ca
Bolton, ON

18013001R00116